Liberating Privilege

The Breakthrough of God and the Persistence of Normality

Liberating Privilege

The Breakthrough of God and the Persistence of Normality

David O. Woodyard

Professor of Religion

Denison University

Winchester, UK
Washington, USA

First published by Circle Books, 2016
Circle Books is an imprint of John Hunt Publishing Ltd., Laurel House, Station Approach,
Alresford, Hants, SO24 9JH, UK
office1@jhpbooks.net
www.johnhuntpublishing.com
www.circle-books.com

For distributor details and how to order please visit the 'Ordering' section on our website.

ISBN: 978 1 78535 462 5
978 1 78535 463 2 (ebook)
Library of Congress Control Number: 2016934233

A CIP catalogue record for this book is available from the British Library.

Design: Stuart Davies

Printed and bound by CPI Group (UK) Ltd, Croydon, CR0 4YY, UK

We operate a distinctive and ethical publishing philosophy in all
areas of our business, from our global network of authors to
production and worldwide distribution.

CONTENTS

To Paul King and Kent Maynard with gratitude for friendship enhanced by their authenticity, integrity, and scholarship.

The existence of the poor attests to the existence of a Godless society, whether one explicitly believes in God or not. This absence of God is present when someone is crying out. The absence of God is present in the poor person. The poor are the presence of the absent God.

Franz J. Hinkelammert quoted in Michelle A. Gonzalez, *A Critical Introduction to Religion in the Americas*, p. 49.

No one gets to reside in Heaven without a letter of recommendation from the homeless... from the dispossessed and disenfranchised of today, who will hold the keys to the future.

Miguel A. De La Torre, in *The Politics of Jesus: A Hispanic Political Theology*, p. 44 and p. 131.

Acknowledgements

Among the joys of being a faculty person are those occasions on which a former student, sometimes a current one, acknowledges that you have made a difference in their life. Often the impact is cerebral; the student has been challenged intellectually to a new level of awareness. Sometimes it is in the form of enabling a student to be free of her/his "inherited wisdom"; to reflect on it critically is liberating. It can be radically personal; one student wrote, "Ten years ago your intervention saved my life and I never thanked you". It can be humorous; one student wrote on a course evaluation, "My first semester in college I really needed a grandfather for a professor". Faculty often shape the lives of student in ways they never imagined.

What is less often recognized is that students shape the lives and careers of faculty. Who we are, how we teach, and the texture of our relationships are a result of the students with whom we interacted. They have become participants in who we have become. While tempted to take full credit for our achievements as scholars, teachers, and advisors the reality is that a student's influence on our careers is substantial. Two that surface boldly are Kelly Brown Douglas, Professor of Religion at Goucher College, and Gary V. Simpson, Senior Pastor at the Concord Baptist Church in Brooklyn. Both are African-American. Once they were my students; today they are my mentors. They (even back then) enabled me to bracket lingering racism and sexism, appreciate my faith tradition with a new lens, and deconstruct my addiction to privilege. And their love over time generated a new sense of self.

Authors tend to take exclusive credit for the production of a book. In reality, the transition from scribblings on yellow pads to documents in a book store requires the labor of many who are invisible. For the initial transition to a computer, enduring the pressure of relentless alterations, and attaining amazing details through the process, I am indebted to Sandy Mead, Erin Lennon, Steven Simpkins and Matt Hughes for "getting it done". Without their generous labors, the book would not make it to book shelves.

College Presidents seldom get the credit they deserve for the careers of faculty. Denison Presidents have made a difference. A. Blair Knapp risked his credibility in appointing this author, then the youngest member of his faculty. A decade and a half after a problematic presidency, Robert Good stabilized the institution and enabled it to move forward. Andrew De Rocco enhanced the intellectual life of the College by instituting an Honors Program and raising the bar on expectations of faculty. Michel Myers contributed significantly to the financial life of the institution and restructured administrative order. Dale Knobel padded the endowment dramatically, enlarged the teaching faculty, and most importantly stressed diversity in the College. Adam Weinberg now consistently acknowledges the contributions of his predecessors while significantly enlarging the horizon of the College. Each provided a safe and stimulating context in which to be a faculty person.

Preface

I grew up and attended church in a village of 65,000 white people; all the ministers were male. Not all residents were visibly rich; none were poor, or so it seemed. If there were persons with inclinations toward their own gender, they were closeted and suffered quietly. It seemed that every father went to work while the mothers cooked, cleaned, and did the laundry. No one talked about privilege, perhaps because no residents seemed without it. At eighteen it was time for college and I enrolled in one with 1199 white students and one African American. Women students were locked up in their dormitories at 10:00 pm and male students were free to roam.

Seminary was next; New York City was different in more ways than traffic congestion! Diligently I read Paul Tillich, Karl Barth, and Reinhold Niebuhr without attention to their disparate worlds to mine. Nothing attached me to the Holocaust, gender and racial discrimination, or the disparity between Wall Street and Harlem. Niebuhr despaired of our indifference to social justice and immunity to its obligations. The library was home, safe and demanding. Then two years in a complacent church did nothing to distract me from my intellectual foci. A college chaplaincy at my *alma mater* fulfilled fantasies of success among privilege, my own as well.

In the late 1960s the Black students were few but fervent. Their intrusion in "happy valley" with a set of demands, in retrospect modest ones, was courageous. Both faculty and students were challenged to stand behind them. Suddenly the writings of James Cone severed my contentment as did his vivid and searching theology; they framed the events and surfaced the issues. The God of the Exodus intruded on the academic quad as She had in former lands. And a decision was inescapable: either back a vulnerable college President who rejected the demands or align oneself with a marginalized minority. Twelve hundred students and thirty-two faculty stepped up to the challenge. An alternate college was formed to replace the one shut down. Finally, the "absentee landlords" (Trustees) arrived to address, some thought tamper with, the Black Demands which the President found offensive. Modest change "trickled down". Several decades later a bold, courageous, and passionate President signed on to the Posse Program which enabled a "full ride" for eighty students of color. Progress, of sorts, finally!

Two years after the Black Demand scenario another book found its way into print: *Beyond Cynicism: The Practice of Hope*. I was aware of being on a different page theologically from former times. Tracing the theological reflections of others was in the past and I was finding my voice. The book was dedicated to a favorite composition Professor whose quirky ways seemed more normal now. After reading it he decoded the document: "David, this may be theology but I see it as about Denison and about you." Apparently, my life and theology had merged. He named a reality of which I was not aware. Liberation theology was on the screen and settled the binary of reflection and action. Marches in Ohio and Washington became nutrients for a new mode of discourse theologically. Three books which were a collaboration with social scientists sharpened the edges of liberation theology yet without revealing an underlying issue: "can a straight, white, male write liberation theology, can privilege be liberated?" Hence, this volume; late but obligatory.

Introduction

The Search for a Center and a Location

It is difficult to dispute the assertion of Walter Brueggemann that we are "all children of the royal (dominant) consciousness." (*The Prophetic Imagination*, p. 39) Some of us were born into it and have difficulty divesting its benefits; others, for whom it is alien, are victimized by it and struggle with preemption and resistance. Straight, white, males, inherently western have been the perpetrators of "othering," yet on the global theological stage are themselves designated "other" as victimizer! And so the question emerges, "How can a straight, white, male do authentic theology when his/her location and centering is the problem?" Some victims are gracious in granting space and credibility to "allies"; but, how does one claim it without dragging into the center the very corrupting DNA which has distorted the faith? Can one tread on sacred territory without inflicting a disruptive footprint upon it? And can we do it without whining? Can privilege be preempted? And then, can one do theology if one has never been in the zone of interlocking oppressions? "…context may not be what is closest to home, but that which needs attending to is 'what hurts' and what lies below the surface" (Joerg Rieger, *Christ and Empire*, p. 7). Specifically, can a straight, white, male make a contribution to liberation theology if he is not hurting in the public sphere?

I

It does not require a very expansive literature review to establish that our mentors did not prepare us for this task. While some embraced the rhetoric of location it was not perceived as an alien and cancerous land; the presumption is we are all the same in different settings. One could search out Paul Tillich, Reinhold Niebuhr, and Karl Barth, among others, without generating a vivid consciousness that we were the enemy, perpetrators of a dominate consciousness that perverted the faith tradition. While we may have been competent there is something amiss in what we did or didn't do; the plague perpetuated by us never rose to consciousness. In a defensive mode, some can remember the distain with which the James Cones, Mary Dalys, and others off the American stage were received by the academic establishment.

How can one do theology when your location is polluted? How can one proceed authentically when one is like the doctor in Albert Camus' *The Plague* who while on a mission to cure the plague was in fact spreading the disease? The claim that "theology should always be written with a pencil" provides some shelter but not enough. The realization we have been writing in ink and legitimizing our inherited wisdom is a stark disclosure but the damage inflicted in the Gospel is beyond integration into our self-regard. We are the "dominant consciousness" in more ways than we can purge readily or acknowledge authentically. Privilege is persistent and normality is foundational! And can it be that the "dispossessed and disenfranchised" have a lock on heavenly chambers? (Miguel A. De La Torre, *The Politics of Jesus: A Hispanic Political Theology*, p. 44 and p. 131).

Surely it is at best disingenuous to blame and vilify our theological ancestors, yet it may be appropriate to identify their deficits. While the language of location and the process of centering are now "the coins of the realm", they are conspicuously absent in most of our forebears. Consider Paul Tillich. He has to remain at some level a theological hero. So many of us would not be in the theological fold without his writings. In an era shaped by the Theatre of the Absurd, the art of Picasso, and the nihilism of some philosophers, we were rescued for the faith tradition by his writings. To righteously distance ourselves from this "giant in the earth" would surely be evidence of faith-fraud writ large. We are here because the writings of Paul Tillich were there. Adolescent purging may create the illusion of adulthood but is evidence of a gracelessness which may for the moment be emotionally satisfying but a "cheap shot", in the language of the street.

Paul Tillich did not use the language of location but a sense of cultural saturation was dominant in his methodology.

> It is not an exaggeration to say the today man (!) experiences his present situation in terms of disruption, self-destruction, meaninglessness, and despair in all realms of life. This experience is expressed in the arts and in literature, conceptualized in existential philosophy, actualized in political cleavages of all kinds, and analyzed in the psychology of the unconscious.
> (*Systematic Theology*, Vol I p. 49)

And Tillich pointed his Union Seminary students to Off-Broadway where the Theatre of the Absurd prevailed, to the Museum of Modern Art where Picasso reigned, and to the offices of the largest collection of psychiatrists in the world. There was a form of location, largely cultural in nature, where many who slipped from the grasp of a faith tradition found an identity. And it was an identity which had a thrust beyond itself. Here we found "a creative interpretation of existence" which seemed real and legitimated a beyond (p. 4). But, consider what is missing. While some would claim "a smile is the same around the world" the location and terms of existence are not.

Paul Tillich did not formally reference a center. But there was one. He wrote in depth about "self relatedness" (p. 169). And it was for Tillich an ontological analysis of a universal self. While the self occupied a time and space it transcended it as well. And it transcended its location in the sense it was ontologically evident over time and everywhere. Gender, geography, time and space did not corrupt its universality. The self was the same "yesterday, today, and tomorrow" and had common elements, three in fact. First, "individuation and participation"; it can both self-separate and engage others. Second, the element of "dynamics and form"; there is passionate intentionality and inherent structures or patterns. Third, the universal self exists in the polarity of "freedom and destiny"; there is the capacity for deliberation and the boundaries of our realities. And "the shock of nonbeing" makes them evident and threatens nonexistence. Eventually this leads to a search for "the courage to be" and the possibility a breakthrough is grounded.

We learned from Paul Tillich's theology there is a necessary rotation between "the eternal truth of its foundation and the temporal situation in which the eternal truth must be received" (p. 3). In time and with his prompts we found ourselves positioned anew in the faith tradition which had lost its hold on us. While Tillich was confident his system was portable, there are no echoes of heteronormality, western imperialism, gender domination, or racial bias to distress us. Yet we would not be in the "theological circle" had Paul Tillich not grasped us and opened up the prospect of a faith tradition. Of course, his and other theologies were written without attention to privilege and marginalization.

To have named our past and disclosed a journey is neither to embrace it as an excuse nor condemn it as a luckless distortion. Our task is to identify it as *there* and move on. Moving on is the hard part! We are still straight, white, males inherently western who are guilty of "othering" and now find ourselves "other" in some measure. We are the perpetrators of privilege and innocence is not an optional self-designation. The context of "what hurts" in the public sphere is not normally ours, unless we seek it. And how would one get "a letter of recommendation from the homeless…"? (Miguel A. De La Torre, *The Politics of Jesus: A Hispanic Political Theology*, p. 44 and p. 131).How does one divest a location? How does one de-center? Those are two different but inseparable questions. Likely it is easier to escape one's comfort zone than shift identities! Yet together they collaborate to define our reality, and that of those less visible and viable.

It does not enable us to imagine a viable center or a purified location when we consider the literature of liberation. Indeed, it is a vociferous and relentless assault on straight, white, males ensconced in the western tradition. We find neither a niche nor an identity on the streets of Peru where the birthing of liberation theology initially surfaced and resulted in Gustavo Gutierrez's classic, *A Theology of Liberation*. We are as whites specifically targeted in James Cone's *A Black Theology of Liberation* and left to wonder if our theology and society have any redeeming qualities. Mary Daly does not conclusively devastate males in *Beyond God the Father* but leaves us in the hopeless reality of the church as she authorizes an exodus. Heterosexuality may be dealt with a bit more gently by John Boswell in *Christianity, Social Tolerance and Homosexuality* but our complicit engagement in heteronormality in time takes a thrashing. Beyond the single hitters on oppression there emerges a collection of double indictments. Kelly Brown Douglas in *The Black Christ* extends the analysis of James Cone to include the oppression of Black Women as a center and location. Queer of color surfaces as a theology, *Queer Theology: Rethinking the Western Body*!, and introduces the multiple forms of homophobia. Before the dust settled on dual oppression, Patrick Cheng identifies "multiplicity" in *Rainbow Theology* which on the one hand embraces multiple oppressions and on the other calls for a transcending umbrella as a unified form of resistance to straight, white, male western realities. Intersectionality sharpens the attack.

The point of the litany above is *not* to establish straight, white, males of western ideologies as the new oppressed! Nor does it legitimate whining as a response. But, the intention is to surface

7

a condition within which we are immersed and which is boldly advocated. What it does do is call for a center and a location other than victimizer. The point is to secure a center and a location which are accessible to liberation and therefore "what hurts".

II

In subtle and significant ways what shivers behind each liberation theology is a narrative, a story of oppression and marginalization. While there are larger narratives, clearly episodes pinpoint the pain. Gustavo Gutierez remembers the confidence with which he embraced his European education and its elegant irrelevance when he walked the streets of Peru as a Priest. James Cone remembers the occasion after his father had appealed to the all-white school board for more funds for black schools – and that night the arrival of the KKK at their doorsteps. Patrick Cheng (*Radical Love* p. IX) recalls, "My early childhood love for God… evaporated in the face of the hatred and intolerance of anti-gay Christians after… [I] started to come out of the closet…" It doesn't require an elaborate narrative to tell the story. Where can a straight, white, male of western origin turn for a story, one that surfaces a condition not his own and a premise alien to his interests?

If one's disposition is first to search the Scriptures a few males come to mind. The disposition to fix on Jesus is enticing but the God dimension is a barrier. Thinking we are god-like is too near the issue for comfort! Perhaps one could step down to Moses whom Hebrew Scripture exalts relentlessly. But the scale of hearing the voice of God and leading a nation toward a promised land creates a sense of foreboding.

There is another story in which we might find a center and recognize a location. It finds expression in five verses early in the Book of Exodus. In the narrative there are no men but that could be a plus! For once we can only watch and listen – which is as uncommon as it is obligatory. Some of us may have heard it in Sunday School but likely did not "get it" really. Patriarchy, like radon, is a silent presence; its privileges are normative and often invisible. The story centers on Pharaoh's daughter and several women who surrounded her. Her father had ordered all male children of Hebrew origin to be tossed into the Nile where survival was impossible. Now there was a "daughter of Levi" (2:1) who had given birth to a son, "a goodly child, (and) she hid him for three months" (2:2). When saving him was no longer an option, she seized a basket and with the child in it "placed it among the reeds at the river's brush" (2:3). The sister of the child observed the impending tragedy and poised for an opportunity to save her infant brother. In time she had one. Pharaoh's daughter "saw the basket among the reeds and sent her maids to fetch it… the babe was crying (and) she took pity on him" (2:6). The sister of the infant seized the moment with the suggestion that she "call you a nurse from the Hebrew women to nurse the child for you." The sister cleverly engaged the infant's mother! The disinherited have to be clever! Pharaoh's daughter took the infant as her son and "named him Moses!" Potentially, the act of compassion had dire consequences. It was nothing like finding a stray animal in the alley and bringing the creature home. "She must cross dangerous societal ethnic boundaries to help regardless of her father's pervasive policy" (Leonardo Boff and Clodovis Boff, *Introducing Liberation Theology*, p. 11-12). A mix of wealth, power, and status did not prompt an act of autonomy. It would be interesting if we knew the story of her being raised in the household of privilege. All we know is that "Pharaoh's daughter is a decisive actor. She works together with other women despite differences of class, nature, and age; she forms alliances" (Laurel A Dykstra, *Set Them Free*, p. 161). The child was saved; he grew up in the Pharaoh's household, and in time departed. And most know the rest of the story of Moses.

There is a story which can identify us a location and there is a figure upon whom to center our existence. Pharaoh's daughter is situated in the center of diabolical power yet able to act independent of it. How she manages to be "in but not of" is not ours to know; somehow she functioned in a location alien to the mission of liberation and managed to be an agent of liberation. You have to wonder if Pharaoh's daughter felt the need to gather Moses in her arms and flee to another location. We will never know – but she didn't! Straight, white, males of western origin might covet the details but their absence means they are ours to craft in our location. For men to become Pharaoh's daughter may be a reach but the courage to embrace her and a willingness to be liberated is the measure of our humanity.

While from liberation theologies we have learned the need to dislocate, Pharaoh's daughter sustained her location in her Father's empire. And there she is the agent of Scripture's premier liberator. In the story she does not flee but stays. But she was not defined by her surroundings. The center held. If a contemporary of ours, she would clearly get "a letter of recommendation…" (Miguel A. De La Torre, *The Politics of Jesus: A Hispanic Political Theology*, p. 44 and p. 131).

III

Laurel Dykstra concludes her introduction to the beginning of the Exodus narrative with the affirmation that the stories are "a dynamic heritage that can help us live our stories" (p. 21). It becomes "the stuff of survival". In this instance Pharaoh's daughter can become a center from which to fashion a theology and contemplate the processes of liberation. Some will be swift to respond that one cannot do theology in "the flesh pots of Egypt". Pharaoh's daughter settled in her location there but was not constrained by it. She acted as one whose center was in purposes other than those of the dominant order. And the rest is history.

If we are to embrace Pharaoh's daughter for the stance of those who were born on the wrong side of the issues and early on embraced them, we need to interrogate her story.

The most obvious insight is that Pharaoh's daughter was not defined by the boundaries of her origin. There appears to be nothing we know in her history which would trigger her response. Likely it was by chance she was on this occasion at the location of oppression. What is to her credit is that she did not look away or flee. Apparently what moved her off her location was compassion. The text reads that "she took pity". "Pity" may not be a word we would prefer but the reality is she allowed herself to feel another's pain even as the order of her Father precluded it. Pharaoh's daughter lived in her feelings of compassion and acted on them.

It is possible that Pharaoh's daughter was tricked into employing Moses' mother as his nurse but the larger truth is that she was open to his sister even if somewhat unwittingly. The least we can claim is that she listened to another woman, perhaps more than one, and embraced a just agenda. In the text there is more "we" language than "I" language. One might be reluctant to give her too much credit but the other prospect is to give her too little. She did allow herself to be prompted by other women and honored their word and support. There is something to be said about being open to being "nudged", having one's impulses magnified.

In a very clear sense Pharaoh's daughter owned her decision and lived with it courageously. She could have passed off the baby and protected herself from recrimination and segregated her emotions. She not only named him (which had more dimension then than now) but she took him as her own. The boldness of that adheres in the fact that the child was not just a helpless baby but a condemned Hebrew child. The reality is that the child was "one of them" and as such, surplus population void of claims. Pharaoh's daughter embraced the unimaginable, undeterred by the risk or the complications. No one, males that is, bothered to record her name.

Yet it has to be acknowledged that in some sense it was not a modest act in a consequential drama. Had the baby not survived and grown into the centerpiece of the Israelite faith and the model of all that followed, likely it would not have been noted or emerged in print. Given that, it is still remarkable she did not stumble over, "what can one do under the circumstance" as many would. There might have been an element of calculation had she known who Moses would in time become. But she didn't. Yet it has to be noted that she did what she could when she could; she became an ally whose act became a magnet for a liberation she could not imagine. At the time it was a modest step, one generated by compassion that was not restrained. It is difficult to imagine what would have happened had she allowed the baby to drown. Aware of it or not, "she is the bridge between the old world and the new" (Hugh R. Page, *Israel's Poetry of Resistance*, p. 261).

Now while feeling another's pain has echoed throughout the consideration it deserves its own attention. When one considers Pharaoh's household, to say nothing of his regime, hardening of the heart is a prerequisite of surviving. The empire not only forecloses compassion but subverts the feelings that lead to it. Everything in her setting and in her primary relationships pointed toward encapsulated feelings of compassion for others not our own. You might wonder how she even explained to her Father the sudden arrival of a child. But she trusted feelings for others and felt their pain into subversive action. When she acted she honored feelings that were forbidden! That commenced a narrative of liberation and action in the sphere of "what hurts".

One thing is clear: we know even less about the development of Moses in his formative years than we do of Jesus. The temple episode is modest but is an indicator positioning Jesus in relation to his identity and mission. With Moses there is a yawning gap between being in a basket at three months old headed to oblivion and his emergence as the centerpiece of Israel's faith – and our own. But, would it not be legitimate to assume his Hebrew mother/nurse did more than birth him? Is it an intrusion on the text to claim she kept him centered in the tragedy and tradition of their people? How else could he have embraced his role in the purposes of God so vividly and consequentially? Apparently with his sister and other servants there was no other access to his destiny in relation to his people. Clearly, all else was hostile to it. Likely that hostility left a mark while his lineage set a course.

It would be a reach to hypothesize the Pharaoh's daughter was a primary agent of a liberative agenda. She could have been but we do not know that. What we do know is that she was there as a surrogate mother invested in the Hebrew child. The simple reality that she never regretted embracing Moses points toward some level of awareness, perhaps endorsement. Over the years she had to be "on stage" in some significant measure. His birth mother/nurse certainly had to have a driving role but it is hard to imagine her nurturing in the Hebrew tradition would be in the shadows. Pharaoh's daughter was really there, both in her Father's realm, and that of the child she claimed as her own. She navigated a dual identity without drowning!

In the language of our day solidarity may be too strong a word. She was not a Hebrew and to moderately identify would have some diminishing consequences. Solidarity often transitions into control. An alternative is in the realm of presence, being in the place of another, alongside. An interesting assertion emerges in the writing of Cynthia D. Moe-Lobeda (*Resisting Structural Evil*, p. 243):"The way in which we perceive the world depends upon who we stand beside as we see it, and whose interpretation we ingest". And it perhaps enables a transition from Pharaoh's daughter to a straight, white, male aspiring to do theology in a liberative mode. To be where it is happening to others is an alliance which perhaps ultimately leads beyond to action. At another time God said to Moses "I have heard the cry of my people". That is where one can begin – not as God! One who is not black, female, homosexual, Asian can be there and hear the cry even if we will never experience the causes. But we can be at their side as we struggle to see worldly realities not our own.

The narrative of our complicity in oppression is bold and inescapable. But it need not tell us who we are or stipulate a need to escape. Pharaoh's daughter is not really a heroic figure but she can be a defining one. Her shadow can hover over and shape who we are and what we can do. She is evidence one can do the right thing while staying in the wrong place! Liberative instances are not to be precluded by privilege. And defined by her center in the midst of a problematic location we can do a theology which defies our DNA, ideologies, and legacy, one authentically bold in resistance. Without being presumptuous or self-congratulatory one can craft a theology from a location it subverts and with an identity of which one need not be ashamed. To the piercing question, "who tells you who you are?" one can say, "Pharaoh's daughter". It is with her in mind, centering who we are, that we turn to imagine a contribution to a theology of liberation from the targeted location, one that created the need for it!

Bibliography

Boff, Leonardo and Boff, Clodovis, *Introduction to Liberation Theology*. (Maryknoll: Orbis, 1980).

Brueggemann, Walter, *The Prophetic Imagination*. (Minneapolis: Fortress Press, 2001).

Cheng, Patrick, *Radical Love*. (New York: Seabury Books, 2011).

Dystra, Laurel, *Set Them Free*. (Maryknoll: Orbis Books, 2002).

Moe-Lobeda, Cynthia, *Resisting Structural Evil*. (Maryknoll: Orbis, 2013).

Page, Hugh R, *Israel's Poetry of Resistance*. (Minneapolis, Fortress Press, 2013).

Rieger, Joerg. *Christ and Empire*. (Minneapolis: Fortress Press, 2007).

Tillich, Paul, *Systematic Theology* Vol I. (Chicago: University of Chicago Press, 1951).

Chapter One

Does God Not Communicate With Us Also?

Some would argue that straight, white, males are wedged into a category boarding on "social junk," "disposable" if not "permanently pigeonholed". To get the Word and speak one is beyond our imagination and capacity. The prospect of ever being on the "right side of history" is even by accident unattainable. Apparently the ability to read the biblical text even in its original language is not sufficient to offset the right context which alone can yield the content. The disposition to do good works may not be sufficient to legitimate them. "The beloved community" is not qualified to formulate the faith or enact it if it is not synonymous with the oppressed ones. And if one is in any way complicit with the empire that is sufficient to invalidate worship and acts of piety. It would seem straight, white, males have no access to the Holy or pretense of legitimate faith. Inevitably, liberation is not an agenda; and a theological contribution is precluded. No "letter of recommendation from the homeless" is likely (Miguel A. De La Torre, *The Politics of Jesus: A Hispanic Political Theology*, p. 44 and p. 131).

We have in the previous section suggested if not a niche there is at least a crevice through which light might escape. To claim kinship with Moses, even as a distant cousin, is presumptuous. To claim an overlap with his sister, Miriam, would seem out of reach. But there is a modest affinity and it protrudes in the 12th chapter of Numbers. While Elisabeth Schussler Fiorenza in *Empowering Memory and Movement* does not advocate that or even hint in that direction, a poaching on her argument might be defensible. In Numbers 12:2 the question of Miriam takes the distinct form of a queering. "Has God not spoken with us also?" Fiorenza notes that "establishment exegesis" is dismissive of

Miriam's question with the suggestion of "privatized sibling rivalry". Of course, Moses is "the sole bearer of revelation" (p. 140). As one struggles through the tangled web of the chapter it seems that "power interests" prevail (p. 141). For the exegetical elite, the case is closed: Moses gets to hear God and Miriam doesn't. When accepting the boundaries of the early chapter of Numbers, that appears inevitable, even justifiable. But, Fiorenza reminds us of an emergent theological tradition which will not settle for confinement. Specifically, "Feminist biblical scholarship has shown that there are at least traces of a different biblical tradition that recognizes Miriam as a prophet of equal rank…" (p. 142). Really, of equal rank? Specifically, consider Exodus 15:19-21, Numbers 20:1-13, and Micah 6:1-8. Here she interprets history and names God's involvement in Israelite experiences of salvation. Miriam is implicated in discerning the role of God and is fully authorized to represent it. Also Miriam is conversant with a "dangerous memory" and clearly is both articulate and author-itative in representing it. Women are not sidelined in access to revelation. There is in her a "democratization" and Miriam is a central figure "in God's saving action" (p. 143). She has heard and she has spoken; Moses has no exclusive claim as an agent of revelation. Consider Exodus 15: 20-21: "then Miriam, the prophetess, the sister of Aaron took a timbrel in her hand… and all the women went out after her. And Miriam sang to them, for he (God) has triumphed gloriously." Authority is not the possession of Moses alone, and his male interpreters. Miriam is not a straight, white, male but she has created a canopy in which we might find shelter, modest legitimacy, even an agenda.

But what if no word is spoken? What if silence prevails and clouds the scene so that neither Moses nor Miriam received auditory signals. That is where the Gospel of Mark takes us in its two final chapters, one elaborate in detail and the other sparse, both haunting in different ways. Having just established a measure of inclusion what if there is an auditory void? Eric J.

Trozzo with a strong nudge from John Caputo and legitimation from Jürgen Moltmann focuses on two silences in Mark (*Rupturing Eschatology: Divine Glory and the Silence of the Cross*). They are "the silence of the cross and the silence of the empty tomb" (p. 41). While inseparable they are distinct, each unique and essential to understanding the divine and justice. Interestingly, these are events in which privilege does not prevail.

Consider first the cross. In the midst of a torturous narrative, attention seems to escape "Jesus' unanswered plea to God" (p. 168). Surely it is grounded in more than physical suffering; while agony has to be a dimension of the cry to God and despair a prominent feature, the reality of injustice undergirds both. "My God, My God, why have you forsaken me?" strikes a chord for which an answer would seem appropriate. The "injustice of imperial power was never present in more vivid colors" (p. 146). However much an answer might seem required, one never came. Silence greets the adorned one. Is that not "cruel and unusual"? Or is it that Jesus never abandoned God and creates an interval for our entry? Could there not be "sounds of silence"?

In an autobiographical reference, Moltmann speaks directly to that. Reflecting on the three years as a prisoner of war, when "religion and theology were totally remote", he came upon "Jesus' cry of abandonment". With Jesus he had cried out, "God where are you?" That is significant for a man who felt no need for one, whose destiny was aimed for the sciences. After reading the text he wrote, "I was profoundly struck... this is the one who understands you... that gave me courage to live" (*In the End – The Beginning*, pp. 34-35). The voice of Jesus was his own.

Then consider the empty tomb. The two Mary's "brought spices" and their agenda was to "anoint" Jesus' body. The 16th and final chapter of Mark is only eight verses while the crucifixion events claimed forty-eight. While they wondered who would "roll away the stone" that blocked access, "they saw that the stone was rolled back". Upon entering they were greeted by a young man, evidently not a disciple and clearly unknown to them. "…He is not here" was the word from the youth, "He has risen". Interestingly it was not the risen one but a word about him and the injunction to go "to Galilee; there you will see him." The two Mary's "fled from the tomb". Apparently not a solemn withdrawal because "trembling and astonishment" prevailed. Because they were afraid "they said nothing to anyone". Now the silence on the cross is paired with the silence which prevailed in the tomb. It was an "awe-filled trembling at the empty tomb" (p. 167). It was "as silence in the face of an iteration of the impossible, of a resurrection moment" (p. 167). Everything is called in question when death is upended.

The Gospel of Mark ends with two silences, distinct but inseparable, both confoundable but certain. And both create space for hope where privilege is not inevitably an impediment. The meaning of the two silences does not hinge on who we are but who the Holy is to us. The breakthrough of God is pivotal and not of our creation.

It would be cruel, even heartless, to obscure the suffering of the cross and the fear of the State's power to execute its will. But to focus on the horror and then indict God for turning a deaf ear would be the result of gliding on the surface of the event. That Jesus was "greatly distressed and troubled" (Mark 14:73) is a given. Jürgen Moltmann in *The Crucified God*, (pp. 150 ff) turns the dial in another direction: "the faithfulness and honor of God in the world" (p. 150) is at stake. "Jesus raises the question, has God abandoned God self?"(p. 151). The dialogue "takes place within God himself" (p. 152). The question of Jesus through Psalm 22:2 and the silence of God are internal to the trinity. It is tempting to suggest Moltmann is identifying a theological exchange! And the queering comes to rest on a "suffering God" who makes the agony of existence the place to be: "the Christ event on the cross is a God event" (p. 205). God is in the suffering of the Son and not separable from it. God is in the injustice of the death of Jesus by crucifixion by the State. And only a suffering God can help. "God allows himself to be crucified... and in this consummates his unconditional love that is full of hope" (p. 248). Breakthroughs are from beyond and generate expectations. They enable us to "abound in hope." (Romans 15:13).

What follows from this is that love and justice are co-mingled in God's accepting space for God self in the suffering of the world and this becomes an invitation. God may be silenced but She will not be sidelined! Our "longing for justice" becomes the opportunity to join God in the worldly places God embraces. The silence of God becomes a call to embrace God where She is in the world and diminish the realm of injustice. God chose the "abyss" over the White House and other elevated thrones and calls us into the "abyss" as partners in solidarity with those who are suffering. Then the silence of God is not a default but an opportunity to participate in a "reversal" (Trozzo, p. 134), a plea "for a release from... the injustices of the world" (p. 190) and a challenge to engage them. The silence of God is a summons to be where God is doing "unconditional love that is so full of hope". The imperial order is put on notice on the cross even as it assumed it had prevailed. And we are to be there. Who is there for us does not discriminate against straight, white, males. The privileged can respond to "what hurts" even if not hurting at the moment.

Then there is the silence that emerges in the empty tomb. Consider it again, the experience of the two Mary's. The young man announced "He has risen, He is not here" (Mark 16:7). Trozzo claims, "The event of a new possibility in the aftermath of the cross is the event harbored in the name 'resurrection,' and resurrection haunts the empty tomb" (p. 151). Consider their response to the non-appearance of the resurrected one. Theirs is a "silent awe" (p. 164). The text says that "trembling and astonishment come upon them" and they were "afraid" (Mark 16:8). And the trembling was so distressful that the ecstasy and awe were so intense that "they said nothing" (16:8). Something so radically new had disrupted their existence and silence was the only option. Horizons of hope overwhelm the "trembling" and flight is the only course of action. Again, Trozzo names the intersection of cross and tomb. One is a "frozen silence" while the other is a "dynamic silence", one frames an unthinkable abyss which is countered and in tension with "the moving, enlivening abyss of the empty tomb (where) a creative force is generated which brings hope that the im-possible may become possible…" (p. 173). And expectation becomes a horizon which counters the silence of the cry of Jesus. The call to justice is validated and authenticated. Hope becomes livable! Something new can happen.

While it may be tempting to settle in and absorb the interaction and interplay of cross and tomb, the silence of dread upset by the silence of expectation, part of the "trembling" of the two Mary's is in the word that "he is going before you to Galilee and there you will see him" (16:7). The significance of that was tapped before. Galilee is the setting of outrageous oppression and of resistance to the imperial order, the order that nailed Jesus to the cross. And Jesus will see you there, in the midst of a counter event which will disrupt the injustice. There the new order will transpire in the strong hold of the old order. Jesus' focus on the Kingdom of God, the coming reign from the future touches down in Galilee. The word from the tomb is to be there, where Jesus is, and the future, is interrupting the status of the prevailing order. We named the claim to be in the midst of Jesus' action in the consideration of the silence on the cross. Now it is a commitment to be there and to join Jesus where he is; the plea to God is answered in the silence of the tomb with the claim to be about what Jesus is doing there. And in the confidence that the God who brought life out of death by being on the cross Herself will prevail and disrupt all the systems, institutions, and ideologies which prevent the future from happening. The risen one is the assurance that justice will override injustice. The longing for justice on the cross is met by the assurance of a future from God certified in the resurrection of Jesus. With Miriam God communicates with no evident restriction when it comes to justice. She apprehends liberation as a Divine act.

I

Previously we contended that those of privilege access to God does not hinge so much on where they are but on who the Holy is to them. And that presses the argument in the direction of the covenant.

When one centers on Exodus events with the lens of privilege, Pharaoh emerges as a point of entry into the narrative. Interestingly, he is never designated by name. Walter Brueggemann suggests it may be because he is a type of which there are numerous incarnations; if you recognize one you know them all. "Pharaoh is clearly a metaphor. He embodies and represents raw, absolute, worldly power" (*Truth Speaks to Power*, pp 16-17). Under his jurisdiction was "the breadbasket of the world" (p. 17). He had "a monopoly on the land and on the food supply" (p. 18). He accumulated great wealth as a result of "cheap labor" and was "propelled by insatiable greed" (p. 19). Despite these privileges he was "consumed with anxiety" which translated into "exploitive work expectations" (p. 20). When it comes to power, a Pharaoh is always the axis on which it turns and at his command. Every empire has one, or more in time. In every imaginable way he orchestrates the economy, and without mercy. Straight, white, males might not feel comfortable with a Pharaoh metaphor for their designation, but it fits in some significant measure. He is privilege personified.

While Pharaoh does not have a name, the leader of the opposition does: Moses whose early destiny was in the chambers of power but whose future was oppositional. Early on in the narrative he is located in the midst of "forced labor" and is the architect of opposition. And in time Pharaoh "sought to kill him" (Exodus 2:15). While we have referenced him as the agent of God to the Israelites, his first real appearance, later he acts boldly in defense of a fellow Israelite who was beaten mercilessly by an Egyptian, apparently for not working aggressively. And Moses kills the agent of Pharaoh. Clearly, "Moses is ready to intervene against the empire on behalf of the exploited" (p. 24). However much Moses may seem "out of reach" as a role model, in reality he is more vulnerable than often assumed.

While to some it might seem to be all about power, it isn't! For two Chapters Yahweh is sidelined in "the crisis of the empire" (p. 22). What was She waiting for? Brueggemann answers "YHWH waited to be summoned by human cries" (p. 23). The crises of pain were an opening in that protests as resistance were taking shape. Yahweh does not intrude in human affairs until there is a historical and human plea. She is not a "helicopter God" who intrudes in ways that preclude human initiatives. The One who was Creator of heaven and earth enters the narrative when Yahweh is invited. God is not Pharaoh writ large! And Yahweh enters as the One who has made promises and honored them. But undergirding that Yahweh is One who *listens*! She "heard the cries". What could be more defining than a God who *listens*? God spoke to Moses but only after God listened. The grounds of hope are there. The promises in creation are legitimated in the Exodus. Thus in Exodus 3:7-9 "I have seen their misery. I have heard their cry. I know their suffering. I have come down to deliver..." Pharaoh's power is now to be subverted. The *listening* God acts in faithfulness.

The Exodus events are the cradle of the covenant. And the covenant is a cipher for who God is. In the biblical tradition, a covenant is not a contract. That tends to be an arrangement between equals. Obligations are legalistically stipulated and enforced. In a covenant, relationality is defining and the framework is the faithfulness of God. She is the one from whom "we receive our very life" (Walter Brueggemann, *The Covenantal Self*, p. 1). God initiates the covenant by faithfulness to promises and that evokes a response to the grace and love. Accountability is response in relationship rather than contractual obligation. Israel remembers the God who *listened* to their cries and lead them through the wilderness and toward a promised land. Deliverance from bondage embodies unforgettable love and grace. Thus, from the Exodus on the Israelites know who they are and the obligation of a received relationship. "When one embraces Yahweh, one embraces not only a very different God, but also membership in a very different social practice" (p. 26). Remembering that God *listened*, and delivered, results in "a genuinely egalitarian community in which... the resources of the community are made available... without privilege or priority" (p. 49). Those who are listened to and acted on are drawn into a relationship in which mimicking defines who they are in relation to each other. Neighbor love follows from Divine love and is inclusive and liberating.

There is no evidence that the Israelites had special merit or were deserving in any binding way. The issue of the Exodus is not hinged on who they are but who God is to them. The viability of straight, white, males rests on a willingness to receive and respond, to be listened to and to listen to others in need. Being heard is binding and liberating, it creates receivership and partnership, and it brackets privilege so the unprivileged can be served. The privileged can enter the narrative because of who is there and what She is about in the world. God does not listen selectively or act in exclusionary ways. While the cries of oppression have a special Divine audibility, the cries of privilege do not fall on deaf ears. And the acts of liberation are uniquely connected to oppression, which does not preclude liberation from the bondage of advantage.

II

To reflect on the Exodus without direct references to hope is to miss the meaning of the event in the life of the Israelites – and ours as well. And it pre-empts the reality of living in the tension between the Cross and the Resurrection. To "abound in hope" (Romans 15:13) is to connect with the One who is "ahead of them in the clouds": Hope is not an attitude or the end result of an emerging trajectory from the past. It is an event from the future! "So God comes to meet men and women out of his future, and in their history reveals to them new, open horizons, which entices them to set forth into the unknown and invite them to the beginning of the new" (Moltmann, *In the End – The Beginning*, p. 87). And the new is not something that evolves in the world but a new reality for the world. Liberation is the future coming toward us!

In his earliest writings Moltmann framed The Christian faith as inherently eschatological. As "the key in which everything is set," (*The Theology of Hope*, p. 16) it is revolutionary and transformative of the present. The divisions of time are reconstructed by the Exodus and the Resurrection events. "The past is the reality which can never be brought back, the future is the potentiality which can never be caught up with, and the present is the interface at which the possibilities of the future are realized or neglected" (*God in a Secular Society*, p. 75). The future from God invades the present and invites correspondence. The God whose essential nature is future penetrates the present (without being present!) in such a way that it has possibilities which are radically new.

The impossible becomes possible precisely because of the contradictions between the promises of God and the realities at hand. Biblical hope is Resurrection hope, the enactment in the present of what is not possible on its terms. And what makes the impossible possible is the faithfulness of God. The location of hope is where suffering is real – where persons are hungry and without shelter, where their dignity is violated even tortured, where they are at the mercy of evil forces over which they have no jurisdiction, and where multiple intersections of oppression are evident. The God of hope is not resident in high places but lowly ones. The Crucified Jesus establishes that location and the Resurrected Jesus opened the future to the radically new. Liberation becomes an option privilege cannot constrain.

And there is nothing in this scenario which precludes the response of straight, white, males. Living God's future is not restrictive but radically possible even among the unlikely. To limit the power of the future to select ones is to deny the capacity of God to bring light out of darkness, to bring life out of death, and the possible out of the impossible. God's credentials are in the Resurrection and God's authority exercised on the Cross. The God who *listens* can create listeners out of those whose hearing is restrained by privilege. The Suffering God may be located with the suffering people but the summons to be there in solidarity can be heard because of the One who speaks.

This calls for a consideration of sin in an eschatological framework. For Moltmann sin and salvation are not hinged on privatized misdeeds, interpersonal slippages, or miscues. Sin is "hopelessness, resignation, inertia and melancholy… in weakness, timidity, weariness, not wanting to be what God requires of us" (The *Theology of Hope*, p. 22). It is the acts or failures in which we shut down the historical opening God has created, despair over the possible over the impossible, forfeiting allegiances to the promises of God. It is not so much what we do but what we don't do; it is abandoning hope and living as if the present is final, fixed, and forsaken by the future; it is living and acting as if the abyss is permanent. And it is at base the failure "to listen to the cries of the suffering poor …and address the concerns that arise from those cries" (Trozzo, p. 65). The God of hope enables the future to shape reality and sin is silence and inactivity. Or one could say it is failure to live in the reality of the Resurrection and taking the Cross as the final word. Sin is a forfeiture of the new creation, abdicating the promise "Behold I make all things new" (Revelations 21:5), accommodation to the present is in the DNA of sin. It is to sidestep the breakthrough of God.

Some like James Cone affirm that sin is a communal concept. Inclusion rather than exclusion is the agenda. Relationality is central. While Moltmann would not reject that, he goes beyond it in calling for the church to be an "Exodus community" (p. 304 ff). It is called to be homeless, never present in ways the society and culture applaud. "Those who hope in Christ..." (p. 21) cannot accommodate or assimilate with established reality. It is the people who cannot put up with the formation of the world because that precludes and preempts the intrusion of the future from God. The people of the Cross and Resurrection seek solidarity with the abyss of the Cross and the contradiction of the Resurrection. They have the future from God and work toward enabling the world to correspond to it.

Perhaps one could call the church the *crucified community*. Its place is in solidarity with the broken and its refusal to embrace the permanence of the present. Solidarity with the future and those tortured by the present is the mission of the crucified community. "Not to be conformed to this world does not mean merely to be transformed in oneself, but to transform the opposition and creative expectation the face of the world in the midst of which one believes, hopes and loves" (p. 330). The goal of the crucified community is to divest the influence of things as they are and to aggressively seek ways to correspond this world to a promised future. The mission is to "fan out" (p. 331) and be in solidarity with "the kingdom of God that is to come" (p. 333). And Moltmann concludes, "To disclose to it the horizon of the future of the crucified Christ is the task of the Christian Church" (p. 338).

The Cross and the Resurrection reveal who God is to us and that contradicts the exclusion of straight, white, males. And we are released from the entrapments not because we may energetically divest but because the crucified community embraces us and shares its liberation from beyond. For a moment at least we are free of being wedged into a category bordering on "social junk," "disposable" if not "permanently pigeonholed". And we have the opportunity to say with Martin Luther King "free at last, free at last, thank God almighty free at last." Normality has been liberated.

Bibliography

Brueggemann, Walter. *The Covenantal Self*: *Exploration in Law and Covenant*. (Minneapolis: Fortress Press, 1999).

Brueggemann, Walter. *Truth Speaks to Power*: *The Countercultural Nature of Scripture*. (Louisville: Westminster John Knox Press, 2013).

Fiorenza, Elisabeth Schüssler. *Empowering Memory and Movement*: *Thinking and Working Across Borders*. (Minneapolis: Fortress Press 2014).

Moltmann, Jürgen. *The Crucified God*: *The Cross of Christ as the Foundation and Criticism of Christian Theology*. (New York: Harper & Row, 1974).

Moltmann Jürgen. *God for a Secular Society*: *The Public Relevance of Theology*. (Minneapolis: Fortress Press, 1999).

Moltmann, Jürgen. *In the End – The Beginning the Life of Hope*. (Minneapolis: Fortress Press, 2007).

Moltmann, Jürgen. *The Theology of Hope*: *On the Ground and the Implications of Christian Eschatology*. (New York: Harper & Row, 1974).

Trozzo, Eric J. *Rupturing Eschatology*: *Divine Glory and the Silence of the Cross*. (Minneapolis: Fortress Press, 2014).

Chapter Two

Straight, White, Males and Heteronormality

Theology has only in recent decades been centered in the queer reality; at its best, it has always been an exercise in queering. When theology forfeits the queer location and abandons the queering agenda the portals for demonic are opened. Authentic theology begins in the crevices of human existence and embraces a "lover's quarrel" with the "normal." Inauthentic theology blends privilege with power and stirs a brew which perverts religion into an endorsement of the interests of the 1%! Queering is always subversive; queer theology is bulwark against the demonic in religiosity and an offense to the *status quo*. "To queer, then, is to *disrupt* the presence of heteronormality…" (Martin Hugo Cordova Quero in, *The Sexual Theologian*, p. 26).

But the question surfaces, can a straight, white, male make a contribution to LGBT theology? Some have claimed that Bill Clinton was our first black President. Dare one claim that a heterosexual male can be a queer theologian? That sounds like a reach, likely because it is. So what can a recovering heterosexual contribute, given a DNA which has been compromised? Not having experienced "what hurts" in this instance, is he decisively sidelined?

In the late 1960s Leroi Jones spoke at a college campus overwhelmingly populated by white students. One brassily asked the author and activist, "What do you want us to do?" He responded "shoot your Mother." Silence prevailed. Eventually a few decoded the message, "You are the problem, fix it not us." The "Master's Tools" are conveniently and comfortably at hand; it seems unlikely that "the eyes of a needle" will yield space for camels to enter. When Scripture has been rendered a weapon of the oppressors; when tradition is loaded with self-interest; and where the institutional church commercializes piety, a theological revision is imperative. Leave it to the least of these commends itself and offers a sigh of relief. Then "shoot your Mother" is an option; purge the blood stream that nourishes the normal.

Peter Berger is a stout ally when he asserts that "religion legitimates so effectively because it relates our precarious world constructions... with ultimate reality" (*The Sacred Canopy*, p. 32). But it also delegitimizes. It recognizes that our sense of reality is no more than "a social construction" and "ultimate reality" rightly conceived is an approximation. At best a straight, white, male can articulate a theology that purges privilege, power, and false gods. He can unmask those who "capture god" and use "him" for their interests; problematize the passages of Scripture that become weapons of hate; and "call out" an institution organized against liberation. Marcella Althaus-Reid calls for an indecent theology "the main function of which is to destabilize the decent order that is a constructed political, social and sexual order which has been ideologically sacralized" (Ken Stone in *The Sexual Theologian*, p. 101). That deconstruction can be an ally to LGBT theology.

Queering and theologizing are "joined at the hip!" Authentic theology is "epistemologically modest", and it approaches the ontological with trepidation. Paul Tillich makes the vexing claim that "no one can call himself a theologian. Every theologian is committed *and* alienated; he is always in faith *and* in doubt and he is never certain which side really prevails." You can't get it right and if you think you have you can be sure you haven't! His grasp of the Christian message is something he/she is "sometimes inclined to attack and to reject it..." (*Systematic Theology*, Volume 1, p.10). Unless one is deluded into thinking he can "capture God," the "normal" is inaccessible. Hence, the French proverb, "A God defined is no God at all." A fully accessible "normal" is idolatrous!

While a straight, white, male with theological interests may not position himself to do LGBT theology, he can "shoot your Mother," surface a kind of prolegomena which closes off the portals for the demonic. Purging the theological "normality" is a heavy task and a necessary one. While straight, white, males cannot create LGBT theology given their location and center, they can contribute significantly to the subversion of heteronormality.

For purposes of clarity perhaps it would be helpful to identify the agendas and actions of two straight, white, males who both happen to be Baptist ministers. They illustrate how a common tradition has been channeled into irreconcilable positions.

On May 13, 2012 Pastor Charles Worley of the Providence Road Baptist Church in Maiden, North Carolina distributed a sermon through the Internet which drew national attention. His proposal on that Sunday was to "build a great big large fence 50 or 100 miles long. Put all the lesbians in there. Fly over and drop some food. Do the same thing with the queers and the homosexuals. Have that fence electrified so they can't get out. You know what, they'll die out. You know why? They can't reproduce." We hardly need explicit access to the form of justification for his proposal. While there are only a handful of relevant texts in Scripture, we can be sure he canonized them and reduced them to propositions. No doubt he drew upon ones that suggest an angry God who does not restrain the impulse to end his creation with a Flood. And one can be confident he stood for the restoration of a moral order that has been compromised by Planned Parenthood, feminists, the ACLU, and hippy-types. The end result is a dramatic proposal to be agents of God's purposes in the world. The action and the belief system are in harmony.

The other straight, white, male Baptist Preacher is Dr. George Williamson whose church is in a small Ohio town ringed by the buildings of a liberal arts college. A different version of the same tradition translates ultimately in the formation of a "welcome and affirming" congregation. Dr. Williamson termed that journey as "the gay/lesbian uprising and the breakthrough of God." It all began somewhat inauspiciously. Over lunch three ministers and their wives met and discussed the church being on the wrong side of the issue. The gay/lesbian pride march was to be in Columbus several weeks hence. They decided to be a presence. Others were given the opportunity to join the six. About twenty did. Soon after that a theology class was dedicated to studying the issue and the issue was before a feminist class. The church council in time took up the concern and eventually a church meeting entertained the proposal to be a "welcoming and affirming" congregation. The motion passed, some were hurt, but a few verses of "The church is one foundation is Jesus Christ our Lord" set the grounds for unity. Unfortunately, the Columbus Baptist Association objected and the Church was disfellow-shiped. The next week several gay/lesbian couples came and sat in the back row. In time they and others came and began to move forward in the pews. Their descent was driven by a different reading of Scripture, the articulation of a liberating God, and a commitment to restore justice in the church and to the world.

Two straight, white, male Baptist ministers imagined themselves involved in "the breakthrough of God" in their time. Obviously there is a need for some serious queering. One agenda leads to radical exclusion and the other to radical inclusion. And in both instances the Bible is agenda-setting.

I

Before examining some defining texts, it is important to be clear about the status of Scripture. How is the document perceived in relation to legitimizing or delegitimizing a position? Most in the Christian community would affirm the centrality of the biblical record; the deciding issue centers around not simply the reading but the nature of its authority. We need to know in what sense it can be seen as "true" and defining. The distinction is between seeing the book as a narrative about the ways of God in human history and the voice of God in infallible words. If it is the voice of God dutifully recorded, then every set of words has to be taken at "face value."

There is a bumper sticker that claims, "God said it and I accept it." And the Holy Spirit is in the mix somewhere insuring mortals get it right. Pastor Worley no doubt believes every word of Scripture is a "Word of God" and has unambiguous authority. He would be endorsed by a letter to the editor in the June 7, 2012 *Columbus Dispatch*, p. A5. "The preponderance of evidence in the Bible is for the sinfulness of homosexuality. Those who think otherwise have to use pretty torturous reasoning to support their belief." Confidence prevails and ambiguity is not entertained.

Dr. Williamson sees the Bible as a narrative about the historical "breakthrough of God" but does not embrace the words of the Bible as God's. One cannot use snippets of Scripture as weapons. But one can use narratives as ciphers which identify places where God did "touch down" with an act of "radical love." Martin Luther King's consistent invoking of the Exodus narrative is a clue to recognizing "the breakthrough of God" occurring in the civil rights movement. Part of this is to indicate that not all of Scripture is authoritative or an incarnation. It took form in culture-bound documents which reflect values and assumptions of their time. What Williamson is doing is separating out what Sallie McFague calls "the demonstrable continuity." Reinhold Niebuhr said years ago that myth tells little lies in order to tell the truth. For Williamson the truth is "the breakthrough of God" in liberating action and that sidelines the lies. The depth of God's desire to be one with us trumps culture-bound reflections of the place of women and the nature of sexuality in biblical times. The grace sidelines other words about women, slaves, and the impure and immoral. Hence, everything in the Bible is not true; the narration is reflected in the time and can be separated from it. Taking the Bible seriously does not ride on the assumption that every text is equally normative or that the text is more than a social construction without mortal footprints.

One of the intellectual engagements for a straight, white, male is to assess biblical texts advanced by persons like Pastor Worley who condemn homosexual acts.

Those convinced that the voice of God is captured in the words of the Bible surface some compelling texts. They support the claim that the Bible is unambiguously heterosexual and clearly designates homosexual relationship as against the purposes and will of God. While the presumption is that a chorus exists, the reality is that there are only five or seven texts. And none represent the position of Jesus. Yet they are stark in their apparent claim. Is not the Sodom and Gomorrah clear enough? God destroyed the cities because men treated strangers "like women." (Genesis 18 and 19) Deuteronomy 23 focuses on prostitution but without a designation of appropriate gender. Leviticus 18:22 is a sharp rejection: "You should not lie with a male or with a woman; it is an abomination." Romans 1:21ff references "men gave up natural relations with women and were consumed with passion for one another…" I Corinthians 1:9 specifically mention "homosexuals" as "unrighteous" who "will not inherit the kingdom of God." I Timothy 1:10 references "sodomites" as "contrary to sound doctrine." It may be a reach to declare "the preponderance of evidence" but what exists is unambiguous in its condemnation of homosexual acts. These texts establish the need for some serious "queering." Our purposes may be served by focusing on two of the most consistently invoked.

Our first task, then, is to subvert the claim that Scripture is clear about homosexual acts. No text surfaces more swiftly than that of Sodom and Gomorrah. Some claim the storyline is straightforward and the outcome decisive. The cities of Sodom and Gomorrah are to be destroyed. Genesis 19 centers on the visit to the home of Lot. It is approached by two angels who are on a mission. The cities merit destruction and they are the agents of the warning. It is interesting to note the timeline. The destruction of the city is determined *before* the episode on which the alleged sexual act transpires!!! The men of the city intervene and during the evening demand that the two strangers be released to them. The immediate intent was "to know them," engage in a sexual relationship. Lot refused but in an act of precarious generosity offered his two virgin daughters as an alternative. No deal. The two angels/strangers were the goal. The mob grew more passionate and somehow the strangers induced Lot and his family to flee. And the city was destroyed. How can one avoid the conclusion that the sin of Sodom and Gomorrah was same sex relationships? Arguments from silence are always problematic but it is curious that there are no women to women relationships in the story. This could be dismissed with reference to the status of women at the time. But it prompted one biblical scholar to ask if there are any references to lesbians in Scripture. Miguel De La Torre (*Reading the Bible From the Margins*) concluded "no reference to lesbians exists in the Hebrew Bible" (p. 99). Hence, one wonders if the Scriptures are clear about same sex relationships, why would only male to male relationships be evident?

That aside, Walter Wink (in *Homosexuality and Christian Faith*) advances the argument that such a gang rape "is not about sex. It is about power" (p. 55). The goal is "humiliation and domination" not pleasure and fulfillment. It does not address the issue of whether loving and consensual relationships can be legitimate between persons of the same sex. So, Wink argues the cities of Sodom and Gomorrah missed the mark and are not relevant to the discussion. But it is not sufficient to pass off the men of the city as engaged in rape. The deeper sin, and the one that defines the event, is inhospitality. "In the biblical world, hospitality meant more than simply being neighborly. ...it was a carefully orchestrated social practice to receive strangers and make them guests" (De La Torre, *Reading the Bible From the Margins*, p. 98). Strangers in biblical times needed for their survival "the protection of an established community" (p. 98). Walter

Brueggemann argues that the issue in Sodom and Gomorrah is "a general disorder of a society organized against God" (*Genesis*, p. 164). The fundamental issue is one of justice and the expectation that the needs of the neighbor will be addressed. The destruction of the cities is a response to moral failures in relation to hospitality. Lot's offer of his daughters was, of course, a perverse form of hospitality. Subsequent references to the story strengthen the argument about inhospitality. Ezekiel identifies the sin of Sodom as a failure to "strengthen the hand of the poor and needy" (16:49ff). In reference to Sodom and Gomorrah Isaiah invokes the claim to "seek justice, reprove the oppressor, judge the orphan, contend for the widow" (1:17). And the closest the New Testament comes in naming Sodom and Gomorrah is a reference (Matt. 10:14-15) in relation to "the mission of the twelve." Another way of disarming the text is to note it is about the failure of a community (and its destruction) rather than individual acts of a sexual nature. The punishment is collective even as the failure is collective. Rather than an indictment of same sex relationships, the Genesis text is "the most atrocious example of inhospitality mentioned in the Scripture of Israel" (Robert A. Gagnon, *The Bible and Homosexual Practice*, p. 90) and has no applicability to the alleged issues of sexuality.

Maria Hanes and Gabriel Moran raise a question that extends the applicability issue, in particular, the confidence a text like Genesis 19 speaks to the issue of same sex relationships. "Can something be condemned if the word for that something does not exist" (in *Homosexuality and Christian Faith*, p. 71)? Did in fact the writers assembled in Genesis have homosexuality in mind? Were they making statements of condemnation? Are we dealing with something that is translatable? Could the writers have had the same thing in mind as the readers and translators now? The word homosexual does not appear until 1869. De La Torres notes (*Reading the Bible From the Margins*, p. 98) "...no equivalent exists in the Hebrew (or Greek) text for the word 'homosexual'!"

Indeed, it is difficult to imagine the validity of condemning something for which you have no word.

While some might reluctantly concede that the Genesis narrative is a problematic weapon in their arsenal, surely a text from the New Testament would enable clarity. And what more viable source than the book of Romans? Is it not the premiere theological statement on most issues? Consider Romans 1:26ff. Paul appears to focus on the "dishonoring" of bodies in unambiguous terms. "...God gave them up to dishonorable passion. Their women exchanged natural relations for unnatural, and the men likewise gave up natural relations with women and were consumed with passion for one another, men committing shameless acts with men..." That nails it, does it not?

The ease with which this text is relocated in the 21st century can be challenged by a "what we know and Paul didn't" argument. While not uniformly acknowledged, the evidence is convincing that sexual orientation is not simply a matter of choice. Evidence mounts that "we were born that way" is a valid assumption. The attraction to one's own gender is part of the reality of gay/lesbian/bisexual. If one embraces the evidence of this then what is "natural" to one time may not be "natural" to another. Given this, we may read Paul differently. What he is addressing then are heterosexuals who engage in homosexual activities. That is "unnatural." Peter Gomes quotes John Boswell to the point: "Paul did not discuss gay persons but only homosexual acts committed by heterosexual persons" (*The Good Book*, p. 157). What is "unnatural" takes on a different meaning when we read Romans through a 21st century lens.

What some would find more convincing is attention to the framework of the Romans chapter; that enables a different "take" on 1:26. Paul is in a sense writing theology rather than ethics or law. Romans "does not begin with a discourse about homosexuality but rather with a thesis against pagan religions that replace created things for the Creator" (De La Torre, *Reading the Bible*

From the Margins, p. 100). Idolatry is the defining issue, the framework of the argument. The number of reasons "God gave them up" is substantial but not the driving issue. They "knew God but did not honor him as God or give thanks to him, but they became futile in their thinking... claiming to be wise they became fools..." (Romans 1:21). The outcome was a worship of the creation not the Creator. The promiscuity evident in hetero-sexuals engaging in homosexual acts is an expression of idols replacing the true God. Same sex relationships as such, where "natural" in a 21st century sense, are not the problem; it is the elevation of the created over the Creator.

Earlier we referenced two Georges – Worley and Williamson – both straight, white, males who by vocation are Baptist ministers. They stand in contrary positions on issues of sexuality and both seek the authority of Scripture to legitimize their interpretations. Our study in these pages has been modest but it should be an instrument for setting boundaries to the uses of the Bible. For different reasons, neither the Genesis story nor the Romans verses provide unambiguous support for George Worley's position. And they enable "the breakthrough of God" to be undeterred by texts which allegedly authorize heterosexuality.

II

There is a second issue a straight, white, male can address and it is the reality of America as an Empire and their complicity. Empire claims and exercises "an integrating, absolute power from a center of domination that ...(sees) itself as the unique and eternal regulator of human relations" (Miguez, *The Practice of Hope*, p. 38). Empire is integrally related to heteronormality. Obviously, heterosexuality and homosexuality can be addressed as freestanding issues. But, like race, gender, and other "rights" issues, they are embedded in and collectively related to a sinister network of power and privilege. Empire is the name for it and queering is in order. Intuitively, Americans are reluctant to see their national life as framed by anything that might be perceived as duplicitous. On one occasion President G.W. Bush was quick to declare, "we are not an empire"; and this was in the midst of acting to establish global jurisdiction. Hardt and Negri refer to empire as "a lack of boundaries. Empire's rule has no limits" (*Empire*, p. xiv). Timothy Parsons identifies it as "naked self-interest" (*The Rule of Empire*, p. 2). Now it may sound as if empire is no more than seizing political jurisdiction. But it is a power base defined by "self-interest" which rules over others. And does so from a concentration of privilege in the few. It is marked by a sense of being indispensable and infallible. And it has the power to prevail. As such it is a "master narrative… (which) fixes everything in its place and gives a place to everything" (Marcella Althaus-Reid and Lisa Isherwood, *The Sexual Theologian*, p. 8). The 2012 political scene defined the reality as the 1% vs. the 99%. The numbers may be off marginally but empire defines who is in control and who has the power to define reality for others. They are "norm-setting." Emile Townes, for example, is on the mark when she claims "Empire is part of black Church life… (white legislators) pass domestic spending cuts that cut the heart out of education, child care, access to healthcare, social security and Medicare and radicalized drug laws…" (*USQR*, p. 76). It has become common to refer to sexuality as the last of the civil right issues. Hopefully that does not imply that the others are solved; what it does affirm is that there is a significant network of victims and a powerful set of victimizers. Empire is at the heart of the realities of oppression in multiple forms. "This eroticized power and control paradigm" must be exorcised in the interests of all (Ellison, *Making Love Just*, p. 16). To echo James Cone, none are free until all are free. The prominence of issues relating to sexuality is not diminished by the recognition it is of a piece with other issues controlled by empire. The realization there are cohorts can be empowering.

If theology is not dealing with the stranglehold of empire, it is not in touch with the reality of our lives, and certainly gay-lesbian existence. At times theology has been seen methodologically as a "top-down" enterprise. In a crude sense, it was a process of identifying the truth and applying it. But this raises the question of who does the naming, how the truth gets recognized, and where the consequences lead. If the victims are to be served it will not be by that process; at least they will not be well served. Where one begins is defining; where you start is crucial for a theology faithful to the biblical tradition. "God passes through the world in the lives of the poor…" (*The Church in the Time of Empire*, p. 52). Hence, the starting location is not an air conditioned library or even a sacred space. As Jon Sobrino writes, "Salvation arises from the weak and the small, from the powerless" (*Where is God?*, p. xix). Their refusal to be subordinated is the ground of hope for a different world, one in which heteronormality has been subverted.

There are a cluster of issues that are gathered up in the marginalized and to isolate them is to diminish their power. They keep us on message and on task. Authentic theology arises from their pain and suffering, not those who inflict it. And it names empire as the collectivity of the privileged whose power creates reality for the victims. Empire embodies and sanctifies "the tyranny of constructed identities" (Elizabeth Stuart in *The Sexual Theologian*, p. 69). While there are those who like to work from theory, the task of authentic theology is to nestle with the victims and nurture the power that comes from coalitions of the powerless.

One of the things theology is called upon to deal with is the degree to which empire has become a religion, or, to put it another way, people are religious about empire. Empire is authorized by its association with ultimacy. The magnet of events and the indoctrination of values get collapsed into "doing God's work" and even "acting on God's behalf." The secular takes on the cover of the sacred. To subvert empire is a prime task of theology – and its community. Power and privilege get enshrined in the sacred and confused with it. And its missionary zeal drives reality. Theology centers on the claim "Rome is not eternal" and an "alternative eternity" is an appropriate form of resistance (Nestor O. Miguez, *The Practice of Hope*, pp. 176 & 178). When the slogan emerged, "God hates fags" that is empire in action. Obviously, God is heterosexual; or, at the least heterosexuals are God's chosen people! It is certainly understandable that those who have been severely wounded by the Christian community will want to sidestep theological issues or certainly rile against them. Yet gay/lesbian/bisexual communities can become allies in the goal of neutering empire. But finally it is a theological issue when God is implicated in empire and it sanctions injustice. Injustices have a headwind because pseudo gods are creating the breeze. Then empire becomes the kingdom of God on earth. Part of the task of theology becomes the retrieval of its symbols from empire's prostitution of them. That is urgent and in the foreground of liberation.

The targeting of empire is a significant agenda but not a sufficient one. When theology "begins from below" and the location of the marginalized, the faith tradition undergoes transformation and distortion. Consider sin as an example. When theology is done from above sin is linked exclusively with personal salvation. It is about the fate or state of the individual. When sin is articulated "from below" it is implicated in social transformation. It is about the formation of the society in relation to justice. Again, Jon Sobrino cuts to the heart of it when he writes that "sin is that which deals death" (*No Salvation Outside the Poor*, p. 83). And in another book he claims that sin is "an economy with no thought for the *oikos*; an arms race with no thought of life; international trade …with no obligation of fairness; the destruction of nature with no thought of Mother earth; manipulated and false information with no thought of truth…" (*Where is*

God?, p. xx). And he might have said, "Marriage with no thought of love between same-sex partners." Sin, then, is communal and salvation is social justice. Empire wants sin to be confined to the private sphere where it cannot be disruptive and contest power and privilege. When viewed from below, sin is the failure to open up spaces for freedom, contributing to keeping others "in their place." And salvation is a communal event where solidarity with the marginalized is an obligatory agenda. Where empire prevails, theology is in collusion with the normative; where empire is contested theology is dangerous and subversive. To claim "Rome is not eternal" is unpatriotic!

Consider also the ways in which grace is disfigured by empire. It sets the boundaries of what is tolerated and in its interest. Grace, then, is permission to live in the confines and in the terms set by the powerful. Receiving grace is acquiescence to the terms of reality determined by empire. It is compliance and submission. Encapsulation and entrapment set the conditional terms within which there is a presumption of freedom. One is free to correspond! When grace is liberated from empire it is radical permission. Theology from below sees grace as the creation of conditions in which a new future is envisioned and resistance to the old regime enacted. This is predicated on the claim that God alone is permanent; all "social constructions" are terminal. History is open. In the 1960s a slogan appeared in the New York City subways which read "the future has been canceled." That is the work of empire. When the location of theology is resistance to empire the slogan is again in the words of MLK "free at last, free at last, thank God almighty free at last." From below the cross and resurrection are not the property of the privileged and the powerful. They stand for the death of what deals death. The empire no longer prevails as you are called and enabled to live in resistance, driven by an "arriving future." Hence, the slogan "the future prevails, now live it!"

The castration of empire is a prime contribution of a straight, white, male to the liberation of the oppressed and marginalized; then the last of these but not the least of these can have a space in community where their love can be honored and where their rights are established.

III

A third issue that a straight, white, male can address is that of power which is the handmaiden of privilege. Within the framework of empire, power is necessary, innocent, and absolute. As such it is integral to order. And the nature of power is the capacity to overpower, to control, and to stipulate the terms within which others negotiate their lives. While Americans experience outrage and anguish in relation to 9/11, and rightly so, what is seldom remembered is that each attack was centered on a location of power – Wall Street, the Pentagon, and the White House. As such it was a "blowback" on economic, military and political power. Each is a form in which we control and define reality for others. This is not to justify the attack but to acknowledge the power factor in them.

So, what has religion to do with this? Former Secretary of State Madeline Albright wrote a book with the revealing title, *The Mighty and the Almighty*. And while she is cautious about endorsing a former President who blended his personal piety with a political agenda, she does affirm the words John Adams wrote to Thomas Jefferson: "Without religion this world would be something not fit to be mentioned in polite company, I mean hell" (p. 65). It is difficult to sustain any distance between the "mighty" and the "almighty" once one has seen power as an instrument of world order. That begs the question formed by William Kristol: "What's wrong with dominance in the service of sound principles and high ideals?" (p. 288). The complicity of the almighty and the mighty calls for a consideration of power, especially the power of God. Given the ability of the privileged to stipulate reality, this has implications for freedom in all its forms, and in gay/lesbian/bisexual ones in particular.

Our agenda theologically needs to focus on the weakness of God rather than the power of something almighty. The goal is not to render God a wimp but as One whose power is in his/her powerlessness. "...theologically the task is to relate God to history and persons within it in more relational and mutual terminology. Restraint of power is a more characteristic mode of God's being" (*The Church in the Time of Empire*, p. 24). The breakthrough of God need not be muscular. Rather than being a supernatural super power the God of Paul offered a mode of relationships in partnership with the claim "God chooses what is weak in the world" (I Corinthian 1:25-26). Hence we are raising the question, what understanding of God would subvert heteronormality and promote an embrace of love in its multiple forms? Our presumption is that if we modify the nature of divine power, the power exerted by the human beings would be re-calibrated. If we are "in the image of God" then a transformation of our self-understanding would necessarily take new forms.

From a Nazi prison camp Dietrich Bonhoeffer wrote, "only a suffering God can help." Given his circumstances as a victim of outrageous evil, one might have expected the invocation of massive intervention. Likely the conventional, perhaps evangelical, would have appealed with ultimate power and the control to bring off a decisive reversal. In that vein, philosopher John D. Caputo (*The Weakness of God*, p. 13) writes: "My idea is to stop thinking about God as a massive ontological power line that provides power to the world, instead thinking of something that short-circuits such power and provides a provocation to the world that is otherwise than power." Caputo is subverting the sense of "sheer power" as the mode of divine activity. The collision between Caputo's power of powerlessness and Bonhoeffer's "suffering God" is stark and defining. What would the consequences be of thinking of God as wounded, indeed as crucified? That would enable us to imagine the breakthrough of God in different forms and places that would indeed by liberating. And what if we understood God as coming to us rather than our coming to some heavenly entity?

In the first instance it would locate God among the lowly rather than the enthroned, among the rejected rather than the privileged, among the vulnerable rather than the secure. If one thinks of the New Testament as a narrative, a play of sorts, one has to be struck by "a cast of outcasts… lost sheep, lost coins, lost prodigal sons, tax collectors, prostitutes, Samaritans, lepers, the lame, the possessed, the children" (Caputo, (*The Weakness of God*, 133). The absence of aristocratic figures is conspicuous! Affluent locations are absent! Privilege is not a marker! Were the story written now the update would be "gays and lesbians, illegal immigrants, unwed mothers, the HIV positives…" There is a striking absence of "well born, well bred, and the well to do…" (Caputo, p. 135). One searches in vain for straight, white, males! And that upends privilege and it transforms power. So, we belong at the margins where God has invested the crucified Christ. The powerful are summoned to forsake their privilege and be among those our society has rejected – along with the One, the God, who has embraced powerlessness as a form of presence. And it would give us an agenda as well as others a companionship. To understand oneself as in the image of a wounded God unmasks privileges and lays bare power in the form of powerlessness. The result is a transformative decentering and a call to service. "…only a lacking, vulnerable being is capable of love… incompleteness is, in a way, higher than completion" (Nestor O. Miguez, *The Practice of Hope*, p. 11). The logic of biblical notions of love is that the powerful become weak and the weak become empowered!

The argument could sound condescending. That is, add the gay/lesbian/bisexuals to our list of characters and mix! But once one neuters privilege and its agent power, then a new sense of inclusion is possible and transformative. With a new sense of the power of powerlessness, straight, white, males can be embraced as allies. And to be an ally is not to add your support but surrender the posture and possibilities formerly taken for granted. Those who take the biblical narrative seriously know that the "cast of characters" is short on those with societal rewards and honors. To be in the story means to withdraw from narratives of power and privilege. True embrace is where the excluded have the love that finds room in their lives for those who are a part of a society that has marginalized them. Then, think about it: who welcomed Jesus and who didn't?

There is at least one more dimension to the "wounded God," the one whose strength is in weakness, whose power is in powerlessness. It is precisely the place where gay and straight can meet and be free to embrace. For the gay/lesbian/bisexual the wounds of God are inviting while for the straight the wounds are interrogating. Here the "loosening up (of) the world" can happen (Caputo, p. 287); here is the "powerless power to melt the hearts that have hardened to keep hope alive when life is hopeless..." (Caputo, p. 16) is present. It is where a victim of power and privilege, what Moltmann called "a crucified God", is welcoming and healing. Here is a God who "knows your pain" because "he is in the midst of it." To be in the image of a wounded God when wounded is more than comforting, that is the ground of hope and the prospect of a new future. Conversely, the straight at the foot of a cross is interrogated. One cannot avoid the question of being the crucifier. What have I done, or left undone, which creates the wounded one? But it is more than a disclosure. It poses the question, what must I do to bring the crucified ones down from the cross? What are the conditions of the society – and the disposition of my heart – which keep others on the cross with Jesus? Hence, it is a moment in which one can divest oneself of the role of victimizer and become one who with love creates space for freedom. In the biblical story, the women at the foot of the cross wept and the soldier declared who was really there. "Surely..." gays and straights can meet in the wounded God and embrace. It would be a new sense of privilege when the LGBT community welcomes and affirms straight, white, males! And then respond to make the world different! Alienated and allies can turn from a world that entraps them each and creates spaces in which all can say "free at last, free at last. Thank God almighty, free at last."

Many decades ago a Yale philosopher described the nature of existentialism as meaning, "Everyone has to take his own bath." Obviously, no one can do it for you. Given the centrality of location in the theological enterprise, it is not done in "midair;" there is little a straight, white, male can do to develop and advance gay/lesbian/bisexual theology. But, he can alter the theological project ("shoot your Mother") in decisive and consequential ways. As a starter, this could mean three things. First, subvert the ways in which Scripture is used to support homophobia. Texts do not necessarily mean what they are presumed to say. Second, expose empire as the embodiment of privilege and power and decimate its claims to order the reality in which others live. Heterosexism is among a family of civil rights issues and "none are free until all are free." Third, given the claim humans are "in the image of God" recalibrate the image so that "the weakness of God" describes the almighty. Then, seeing ourselves in a different mirror, victim and victimizer can embrace and together forge a new world order, or at least a new normal! Theology can render heteronormality soluble.

Bibliography

Albright, Madeline. *The Mighty and the Almighty*. (New York: Harper Perennial, 2006).

Althaus-Reid, Marcella and Isherwood, Lisa (ed.). *The Sexual Theologian*. (London: T&T Clark International, 2004).

Berger, Peter. *The Sacred Canopy*. (New York: Doubleday and Company, 1969).

Brueggemann, Walter. *Genesis*. (Atlanta: John Knox Press, 1982).

Caputo, John D. *The Weakness of God*. (Bloomington: The Indiana Press, 2006).

De La Torre, Miguel A. *Reading the Bible From the Margins*. (Maryknoll: Orbis Books, 2004).

Ellison, Marvin Mahan. *Making Love Just*. (Minneapolis: Fortress Press, 2012).

Gagnon, Robert A. *The Bible and Homosexual Practice*. (Nashville: The Abington Press, 2001).

Gomes, Peter J. *The Good Book*. (New York: William Morrow and Company, 1996).

Miguez, Nestor O. *The Practice of Hope*. (Minneapolis: Fortress Press, 2012).

Parsons, Timothy. *The Rule of Empire*. (New York: Oxford University Press, 2010).

Sobrino, Jon. *No Salvation Outside the Poor*. (Maryknoll: Orbis Books, 2008).

Sobrino, Jon. *Where is God?* (Maryknoll: Orbis Books, 2004).

Tillich, Paul. *Systematic Theology*, Vol. 1. (Chicago: The University of Chicago Press, 1951).

Townes, Emile M. "Responses to 'New Testament and Roman Empire'." (USQR, Volume 59, 2005).

Wink, Walter. *Homosexuality and Christian Faith*. (Minneapolis: Fortress Press, 1999).

Woodyard, David O. *The Church in the Time of Empire*. (Winchester, UK: Circle Books, 2011).

Chapter Three

Economic Privilege, Complicity, and Liberation

In the rotunda of Union Theological Seminary Reinhold Niebuhr said to a cluster of gaping students: "With bluster we critique capitalism in these halls while we are living off it as an institution". We might aspire to a cleansing of its permeation of our social existence, but ideological virginity is not an option. Targeting the market as the perpetrator of injustice may be a valiant agenda but it is exercised in an environment it saturates. Modifying consumption is a noble exercise but controlling desire and greed does not purge the system of pollutants. Certainly one can refuse to pay taxes that support the military industrial complex but they also support essential social programs. An academic can boast that he/she does not own any stocks but the pension plan insures complicity. A church can proclaim that "politics and economics don't mix" but hardly a penny is pledged that is not generated in the economic system. Every effort to echo with Martin Luther King, "Free at last, free at last, thank God almighty we're free at last" is a worthy aspiration but at base is a fiction in relation to the economy. An economic order can make privilege permanent, or nearly so. It certifies normality.

Straight, white, male does not exist in a vacuum; the triangle and the privilege positioned by an economic system exacerbates advantages and sustains them unambiguously. And contrary to popular belief the economy and religion are ubiquitous bedfellows. Of the postures that define their relationship, perhaps the most dangerous, is when the economy takes on the features of a religion. That alliance among other things often sets the economy in a sphere where criticism is indefensible, especially when both are blended with a version of democracy.

The privileges of straight, white, males are enhanced by their economic foundation, often celebrated in religion-like rituals and creeds. The triangle is not economically neutered, or religiously neutral. There is at least some validity to the claim that as the economy is under surveillance, religion can't be far behind! It may be revealing to highlight some models of the interpenetration of religion and economics which sustain and enable privilege or challenge it. Versions of the Divine are in full evidence, stealthily so.

I

One of the first models to slither to the surface is the prosperity gospel. The "tag" may not protrude in the public consciousness but it is difficult to miss the preaching on the T.V. screen. While Joel Olsteen may not be associated with the designation, any scanning of the screen eventually centers on his inviting smile, three-piece suit, and message of good things to come – all from God and to the deserving. The underlying promise is "that God's favor is shown to believers in an immediate, material way" (Stephanie Mitchem, *Name It and Claim It* p ix). And fulfillment is a blend of authentic promises from a faithful God augmented by an aspiring and energetic embrace of it. It is a give and take covenant of enduring validity.

While the black community and church is not uniquely susceptible to the prosperity gospel its focus on the body in some measure assures vulnerability. African Americans have a strategic position in the recognition we not only have bodies but are bodies. Kelly Brown Douglas exposes how "the narrative of civility" has corrupted the black churches' care of the body; yet its centrality cannot be disputed. While only a modest amount of imagination is required to focus on what the white community has inflicted on the African American body, it is not difficult to imagine why "the black church is a body centered church" (*Black*

Bodies and the Black Church, p. 74). "The disrespect of black bodies has been the hallmark of oppression" (p. 76). It is not surprising therefore, that material advancement would capture attention. And the prosperity gospel secures a place in the nature of the black church which at best is a "home for black bodies" (p. 168). The Gospel gets translated into "God's favor... in an immediate, material way". With the vulnerability of the body and its centrality, aspirations to privilege are compelling and beyond resistance. Piety is justly rewarded, or so it is proclaimed. A commercialized Christianity is irresistible!

The prosperity gospel may be conspicuously focused on the African American community but not exclusively so. In a sense what marks off the prosperity God is a significant shift in the texture of "the promised land". It is not so convincingly political as it is economic. While the civil rights movement was self-evidently focused on political freedom, one should remember that Martin Luther King was assassinated after a day in which he marched with workers seeking economic deliverance. This is not to associate King with the prosperity gospel but to recognize a cultural shift toward economic deliverance. The God of the prosperity gospel alters life now, not in some distant orbit. Upward mobility is an aspiration initiated by a God who is embodied in historical circumstances. Somewhat simplistically stated, God's agenda is for us to be better off. And if you give you get! "Some ministers confidently promised a one hundred-fold return on donations to their organizations" (Kate Bowler, *Blessed* p. 53). And she quotes Kenneth Copeland as proclaiming, "The gospel of the poor is that Jesus has come and they don't have to be poor anymore" (p. 77). Acts of faith and financial advancement are interrelated. God has a plan for your wallet, if you do your part of giving and striving abundant rewards will accrue. The return on a tithe can be astronomical! One church even offers "a money back guarantee" on a tithe (p. 99). Apparently the church and the marketplace have merged. Again, give and get are correlated and assurances come from God backed by the church. Capitalism is the good fortune of Christianity.

The temptation might be to dismiss the prosperity gospel as a fluke, aberration, which could not remotely be associated with a serious explanation of religion and the economy, of privilege and oppression. While its detractors may be offset by its millions of adherents, one might venture the claim that in the American ideology success and faithfulness are not so visibly disconnected. Kate Bowler concludes her judicious studies with the observation that "People wanted churches that lifted their gaze, enlivened their spirits, and assured them that help was around the corner" (p. 257). Was not the Exodus narrative an economic as well as a political event? The labor force was liberated and an unjust economy imperiled; "help was around the corner;" actually, it was ahead of them "in the clouds". In later times at least a fraction of Weber's observation was that capitalism thrived where Protestantism prevailed. The purposes of God and the aspirations of humankind are admirably related, perhaps deviously intertwined. The breakthrough of God is prosperity.

II

While the prosperity gospel conflates religion and the economy, Michael Novak and his ilk find them convincingly in harmony. Novak aspired to a lasting career in the academy, yet he yielded to the call to be an advisor to President Reagan and eventually a principle in the American Enterprise Institute. There he managed to negotiate a harmony between the two realms, and a relationship of mutual benefit. While clearly differentiating himself from the boldness of recent Catholic social teaching on the economy and its decisive radical bent, Novak lauds democratic capitalism as having "revolutionized ordinary expectations of human life" (*The Spirit of Democratic Capitalism*, p. 13). The benefits are astronomical. The market economy facilitates the rights of life, liberty, and the pursuit of happiness even as it provides the condition of prosperity for all. A market economy and political democracy are not incidental bedmates but inherently and irrevocably linked. They are not simply compatible but inevitably co-exist and thrive. Novak does not exonerate that economic order but simply affirms there is none to compare: "Democratic capitalism is neither the Kingdom of God nor without sin. Yet all known systems of political economy are worse" (p. 28). For Novak that is more than faint praise. The Kingdom of God may not have secured in the economy a perfect fit but it certainly is a convenient one. Perhaps one could say it is providence-lite!

Novak at many points seems to trail the argument of Adam Smith in the claim the market is a complete system. It does not seek or aspire to appendages which would purify or even enhance its actions. This is not to suggest it is a perfect system. While Novak is confident "in the evidence of the immense benefits in the form of prosperity, liberty, and significant moral progress that the capitalistic economy ushered into history" (in Peter Berger, *The Capitalist Spirit*, p. 52) it is not stoutly virtuous as a system. What in a sense "saves the day" is the "invisible hand" inherent in the market. In a sense, the system has a gracious will of its own. But that still requires a cohort. Humankind is created to be embodied and fulfilled in the historical order. While acknowledging a monastic and other-world tradition, "Christianity also has a this-worldly, bodily, incarnational side.... Christians are properly at home in the flesh, in their world and in the struggles of history to build up a Kingdom of truth, justice, love, and beauty..." (p. 55). For Novak, Christians are obligated in their daily life to image their Creator. This is the sphere of accountability and their passionate engagement with activity in the world is under surveillance. And in particular, "the drive to better one's condition is not evil but good" (p. 73). Even as God is a Creator, mortals are under orders to create systems that lead to the production of wealth. This enterprise is not self-indulgence or driven by greed but the obligation to use the resources provided by God to enhance human well-being. For Novak, "economic development has become a moral obligation" (p. 79). To be enterprising – in several senses of the word – is to be faithful to the gifts of our Creator. Hence, the development of the economy is a moral task for which one is accountable ultimately. It may seem too simplistic to say it, but, God wants us to be successful in the world and that is what creates wealth and prosperity for all. Grace and wealth are conflated. To paraphrase T.S. Elliot, "God likes giving, man [sic] likes getting; the economy is admirably arranged." It is here and now that mortals are accountable for the production of wealth as well as the just use of it. Neither Novak nor Smith is a disciple of Max Weber but there are some echoes and this is one. One has to be reminded that there is an "eschatological tow" (p. 54). Fruition is not simply a consequence of human passion and focus. Providence has a pull in history toward a future in the purposes of God.

This positions us to consider "the invisible hand" popularized by Adam Smith. Michael Novak strives to diminish the force of this image. While it has assumed the status of a defining and monumental reality, he notes that it only appears twice in Smith's writings, "each time briefly and glancingly.... It enters the discourse casually" (*The Spirit of Democratic Capitalism*, p. 113). Novak claims that "the metaphor, simply put, draws attention to unintended consequences" (p. 114). All that it really does is affirm that there is an order and the choice of individuals within it create outcomes; he claims that the hand is nonexistent (p. 115). Coercion is not at play. It is simply how it works when there is order, liberty and human striving. In the measure providence might be seen as a transcendent factor, it would be really a more secular providence – the way things work. What are the "unintended consequences"? The eventual outcome is that the self-interest of individuals will in time result in a benefit to others. Apparently there are self-regulating powers which promote the welfare of all. Joerg Rieger in *No Rising Tide*, (p. 65) quotes Smith as claiming that an individual "led by an invisible hand to promote an end which is no part of his intention" will secure outcomes in economic prosperity independent of any design in his/her part. By some mysterious and unintended process, selfishness results in altruism! The invisible hand is not an ontological reality but how the system works – unless it is tampered with.

It would seem that in the effort to neutralize any sense of coercion by a transcendent entity Novak and Smith have preempted a role for religion; however, that would be an unlikely agenda for a Catholic Theologian! Novak dispels that interpretation. For Novak if not for Smith God is not one who manages the outcomes of the market; however, the Holy Spirit is complicit in the creation of the system itself. There is a semblance of embodiment. To say that democratic capitalism is sacred territory would be a distortion. Novak repeatedly acknowledges significant flaws but the system itself has an origin not of human construction. The Holy Spirit is complicit in the sense of creating an order which can produce unintended consequences. In a sense, while the "hand" does not exist the results ascribed to it are a result of a system which is the territory of the Holy Spirit.

The closing words of *The Spirit of Democratic Capitalism* do not see it as created in the heavens, but they do suggest some system agenda-setting. "Almighty God did not make creation coercive, but designed it as an arena of liberty. Within this arena, God has called for individuals and people to live according to his law and inspiration. Democratic capitalism… created a non-coercive society as an arena of liberty…" (pp. 359-360). Apparently, God wired the system!

Some might be tempted to draw lines between the prosperity

gospel and the work of Michael Novak. There is some overlap in that both fearlessly authorize an alliance between religion and economy. But not the same one. For the prosperity gospel the focus is in how you get what you are entitled to. It's give to get in some sense. God has a material agenda for those who claim it. For Novak democratic capitalism is an order which points towards a community in which all benefit from the initiatives of individual persons. There is a difference between intended and unintended consequences. The outcomes are radically different. The one focuses on how an individual may secure benefits and the other how the result of self-interest translated into social goods, to the benefit of all. While Novak repeatedly baptizes the economic order, the prosperity gospel advocates exploiting it; both positions are sanctioned by Christianity.

While Novak is clear about human responsibility for others, it would seem he is not self-conscious about privilege. It is something readily available and the only sin is to use accumulated wealth in ways alien to the purposes of God. In no sense does Novak acknowledge that aspect of privilege which clouds vision and sustains purposes at odds with those of God. Paradoxically, the deserving earn what they have been given! The alleged breakthrough of God could be celebrated in the sanctity of Wall Street.

III

Gustavo Gutierrez shares with Michael Novak an allegiance to the Catholic tradition but in relation to economic issues it is not the same one! While the Peruvian priest meticulously documents his writings in Catholic social teaching, Novak paints with a wider brush, one that covers and some would say covers over. Novak does not deify democratic capitalism but Gutierrez tends to demonize it. Their locations could not be more dissimilar. As Novak paced in the halls of the White House and then became

enthroned in The American Enterprise Institute, Gutierrez minis-
tered on the streets of Peru! The consequences for their writings
are conflicting and irreconcilable. For Novak, Christianity and
the economy are congenial while for Gutierrez Christianity
requires a divestiture of engagement. The one is at war with
socialism and the other at war with capitalism. And Christianity
is a player on both courts! Novak courts privilege while Gutierrez
demonizes it. For Novak the system provides opportunities for
material gains; for Gutierrez it prevents human flourishing.

Although Gutierrez is quite explicit in his rejection of
capitalism it would be a mistake to begin directly with that move.
One needs to begin where he does and it is not initially with
systems and ideologies. As noted earlier, he returned to Peru
armed with a carefully groomed doctorate – in the European
tradition. But the setting on the streets of Peru disassembled its
validity. What he had thought and researched was from another
world, one content to hold privilege accountable but not
problematic in itself. Ambiguity is not a compelling category for
Novak. The God of the faith had at best restrained postures in
relation to the realities of the lives Gutierrez encountered on the
streets. That became the axis for a theological revolution. And it
began craftily with those who were the victims of privilege, those
for whom privilege has been preempted.

When Gutierrez talks about "The presence of the absent ones"
(*The Density of the Present*, p. 125) it may well initially sound like
a carillon call. But the victimizers are called to listen to the silent
ones; it is in the silences that voices can be heard! And what
marks their existence is "a state of hunger and exploitation, insufficient health care, lack of decent housing, difficult access to
schooling, low wages and unemployment, struggle for rights and
oppression" (*The Truth Shall Make You Free*, p. 10).Their days are
marked by "institutionalized violence" but passivity is not their
response. There is an "irruption of the poor", those who have
been absent are becoming present (p. 8). To be even more specific,

"the poor have begun to see themselves as the subjects of their own histories and have begun to take their destiny into their own hands" (*The Density of the Present*, p. 125). Those de-privileged by the systems of the world are now claiming their rights to a life in the world where they can flourish as human beings. It is clear to Gutierrez that these "anonymous ones" have recognized that their problem is "the very logic of the system" (*The Power of the Poor in History*, p. 117). Their neglect has an origin and it is not in their willingness to be victims. The nature of the economic system is inherently an agent of victimization. Their non-privilege status is a result of structure and not simply human frailties. Unfortunately, a popular religiosity which turns its energy inward is complicit. There is a dominant theology which focuses upon inferiority and explicitly engenders a transgendering effect on the faith tradition. And the consequence is that the dominant order can escape rebellion by virtue of reform and adjustments to the mechanism of distribution.

But the "irruption of the poor" is not a passing phase which will be soothed by acts of charity. Imbedded in the struggle to be present in history is a "God [who] has a preferential love for the poor and dispossessed" (*The Truth Shall Make You Free*, p. 14). Indeed, "the God of the Bible irrupts into history" (*The God of Life*, p. 27). Clearly it is a breakthrough from beyond. Even as the God of Israel was pitted against the political/economic order in Egypt which made slaves of the Israelites, so that God is in union with "the irruption of the poor" and granting persistence to the rebellion against the economic system. God is in a covenantal relationship to the poor and marginalized now as God was in the Exodus. God does not substitute God's purposes for the action of the poor but empowers them. The irruption of the poor does not ride alone on its own determination but is gathered up in the freedom struggle of the God whose faithfulness has warranted struggles for freedom through the ages. The system will not prevail. Structures which benefit the few and oppress the many cannot withstand the workings of God in history on behalf of the "anonymous ones". God is partisan and it is not with the privileged.

Certainly Gutiérrez acknowledges that Christianity has been complicit with capitalism. But the God of Moses and Jesus Christ is in covenant with a people who have recognized the systemic poverty and are in rebellion against this system which sustains it and originated it. The theology of liberation identified with Gustavo Gutiérrez beginning in the victims of capitalism and then God both "heard their cry" and promised to be "ahead of them in the clouds". The Promised Land is not an alliance with "The Spirit of Democratic Capitalism" in any manner, shape, or form.

This concludes the summary of three models for envisioning the relationship of economics and religion. And when each of the three formations yield to the issue of privilege their spread is apparent. For the prosperity gospel the economic order can be played for privilege and religion provides the assurance of an unambiguous bargaining chip. For Michael Novak the economic order is the portal to privilege and the faith tradition is complicit in the creation of the system. For Gustavo Gutierrez the economic order is the servant of the privileged and the faith tradition with its God stands in unambiguous resistance. The breakthrough of God is in a conspiracy for justice, the demise of privilege, and love cavorting with justice.

IV

While the rendering of these three positions may have been stealthily generous, biases were likely evident. The third argument for some is the most compelling but the search for a better way of relating religion and economics agitates for an attempt. Is there a way of relating, in particular, Christianity and capitalism which subverts privileges at least modestly and restrains the position of straight/white/males? One place to begin would be an amplification of a claim certified earlier, namely, that the economic order has become a religion. Christianity is no longer a player in this scenario, at least not in any doctrinal sense.

It has to be somewhat compelling when a social scientist refers to the economy as "a powerful secular religion" (Robert H. Nelson, *Economics as Religion*, p. xx) and a theologian refers to "the hidden theology behind the religious economic order" (Jung Mo Sung, *Desire, Market and Religion*, p. xi). They converge in Nelson's contention that "specifically theological assumptions are not foreign to economic life or economic thought, but pervade them" (p. xiii). In the mix the designation "secular" is not too difficult to decode: of and in this world and nothing beyond it. In short, there is nothing more than here and now. The heavens are for clouds and spacecraft not deities! The designation "religion" may be somewhat more obtuse! It would not be a reach to suggest it is marked by trust in something ultimate (or indisputable); having explicit and confident assumptions or claims; articulated in creedal forms and celebrated in rituals; and translatable in ethical/moral behaviors and norms. There is, then, in economic ordering a "hidden theology" embedded in systems and institutions. In a real sense, economics is elevated when it functions as a religion, less subject to dispute, and more sustainable. And, as we will argue, more generous in advancing privilege. De-sacralizing is in order!

The dimensions of the problem of economics as a religion become clearer as the consequences of a particular market system surface. When one of the nation's wealthiest investors announces he pays less taxes than his secretary inequity emerges without much ambiguity. On a global level a United Nations research agency indicated that in the year 2000 85% of assets where owned by one tenth of the adult population. While this is global and not exclusively a function of capitalism, the economic disparity in 2007 was evident in America as it was revealed that 10% of the population owns roughly 43% of the wealth and 7% is owned by the bottom 80% (Cynthia D. Moe-Lobeda, *Resisting Structural Evil*, pp. 33-34). It has become more common currently to talk about the 1% and the 99%. While something of a slogan it represents the reality that this economic order has raised privilege to a new level. The disparity is called by some "economic violence". One of the ways to visualize the extent of disparity is to calculate the transformation in compensation over time. The CEO of companies in 2006 made 364 times the compensation of a worker. And more starkly, "The difference between the salary of an average worker and the top twenty private-equity and hedge fund managers... [is] 22,255 times the pay of the average worker" (Joerg Reiger, *No Rising Tide*, p. 9).

The claim that the economy has become a religion is not difficult to articulate with more specificity. That a form of theology pervades the capitalist order is evident on every count. Consider that the market itself has become an ultimate, an indisputable certainty beyond criticism. It is the new transcendent that reigns and defines reality. And the economists form a priesthood that assures the sanctity of the order. The existence of adoring rituals is nowhere more evident than at 4:30 when Wall Street closes the market with a pope and cardinals presiding. The creed of individualism and the rights of liberty prevail and clarify the centrality of self-interest. Clearly salvation clusters around the accumulation of wealth and sin is deviation from that agenda. The norms of the economy structure the moral authority of the culture and achieve a stature that is beyond judgment. The market economy has created a paradise for some, perhaps only a few, and their power to ensure their privileges is indisputable. It is difficult to imagine becoming more religious. No wonder the assertion emerged that "economics is too important to leave to the economists" (Steven Keen, quoted in Joerg Rieger, *No Rising Tide*, p. 3).

A thoughtful consideration of the market-based economy

identifies the dimension of desire, the ways in which it exasperates and is transformative. Typically those immersed in the economic order do not submit this to sustained critique. It is there and essential to progress. While desires are often unconscious that only serves to identify their vulnerability. At the simplest level, needs become desires and their magnification is often beyond control. At the mercy of the market: "Desire is not aimed at a pearl necklace in and of itself… but at the related hope for greater self-confidence and even love" (Rieger, p. 96). And that fuels the economy in radical forms. Once needs become desires they are produced and get to be instruments of profit; then the system rolls and free choice is radically abridged. The significance of this is that: "In capitalism the desire for having has become not only central but almost total" (Sung, *Desire, Market, and Religion*, p. 48). There is very little that desire does not trump; it has a death grip on the reality within which one lives. The market feeds on it, is fed by it, and in the process persons are commodified. In the words of Daniel Bell, "the capitalist economy of desire is a manifestation of sin because it both corrupts desire and obstructs communion!" (*The Economy of Desire*, p. 89).

It may not seem that straight, white, males have any inherent relationship to privilege in the market. But, it simply is the case that this is where they are in abundance! Consider the scene at 4:30 on Wall Street, peruse the glitzy stockholder reports complete with "portraits" of the Board, glare at the collage of CEOs on the bank rosters, read "The Wall Street Journal" and magazines like "Fortune", then search for articles by non-white males and it becomes evident who is on the throne. The winners are on display. Absent evidence of straight, it is a "slam dunk" on who reigns. And who is incidental!

A secular lens may not want to give religion the prominence being argued. When one sets that aside the reality is that in the *status quo* very little seems provisional. Whether or not the category of absolute is desirable, absolutizing seems to be a rather clear phenomenon. Some would say that it is easier to imagine the end of the world than the transformation of it. In the tunnels of New York City subways about six decades ago a slogan frequently claimed the walls: "The future has been cancelled." The economy in particular seems to be a subset of an unimaginable new order. It is somewhat like an odorless gas which is present but not perceivable. Like radon, it comes from the foundation and creates an unfavorable environment. Powerlessness does not seem likely to be reversed in the face of the "way things are" economically. The good life for some will always be at the expense of the majority. A transcendent fix seems as likely as a revolution. The heavens are as empty as the corporate elite are impenetrable. A course in business ethics seems as impotent as a divine teddy bear. A rising tide sinks all boats except for a few corporate battleships.

There are dimensions of the metaphor crafted by John F. Kennedy one can salvage even as subverting its affirmation is agenda-setting. The most obvious recognition is that we are all in the water and a worst case scenario is that the water is inhaled to the point of extinction. We have to survive, swim, in an environment that is reality-creating while resisting the tide, even swimming upstream. The market economy is unlikely to self-destruct even as the waters are unlikely to evaporate. To be perhaps overly playful, Gustavo Gutierrez wants to walk on water until society reaches dry land. Likely that eventuality is easier to imagine from the Third World than the first one. Realistically, the market economy has at least a provisional permanence. It is not where we belong but it is where we need to be. And we have to reckon with the realization it authenticates and sustains the very privilege we are concerned to abort. So, the issue becomes: how does one keep from drowning while resisting the tide and not be trapped into endorsing something detrimental to human flourishing?

While the above borders on a "counsel of despair", in reality elements of light pierce the darkness. There is an illumination of where action needs to emerge. Joerg Rieger is on the mark again when he writes, "we need to make sure that economics and religion deal again with the reality that hurts" (p. 28). It may be tempting to wrestle with economic theory or creedal formulations but hope for a new future resides in the hopeless ones and "the reality that hurts". They have access to reality in dimensions inaccessible to the privileged. Gustavo Gutierrez is prophetic when he writes about "the power of the powerless". The victims see what the victimizer glazes over. The Catholic bishops affirmed "the hermeneutical privilege of the poor"; they see the radon! And eradication becomes an option. They have perceived the truth because they have lived in it.

Then, consider this: if one elects to live in the truth embodied in the Jesus event it is clear the poor is the place to be! Marginization is his reality and the reality of those he sought. Clearly he got off to a problematic inception; he was born in a manger to an unwed Mother with a Father who was not a factor in conception and who seems to fade out of the narrative. Shepherds were prominent attendees but they rated a minus ten on the social scale. Jesus distanced himself from his tribe in the temple at a distinctly young age. He returned to announce, with the benefit of the prophet Isaiah, that he is committed to "good news for the poor". In his ministry he focused on tax collectors, lepers, prostitutes, and others whose insignificance was astronomical. He had the audacity to claim in his preaching that God not only privileges the poor but is integrally allied with their interests. At the same time he is brutal in reference to the rich. In Luke 12:16-21 he makes bold to expose the folly of the rich in thinking they have secured their future by accumulation and in Luke 14:12-13 admonished a host to fashion a guest list of the poor and disabled while ignoring his own class. To know God is to be inseparable from solidarity with the poor. That is where

God "hangs out". In every sense Jesus' focus is on "the human being who is not considered human by the present sacred order". (Gustavo Gutierrez, *The Power of the Poor in History*, p. 193) Jesus certainly would not have passed Temple 101! And he is ultimately rewarded for being unpatriotic by crucifixion by the state. Only women were at the foot of the cross, and they were by gender marginalized; none made the cut for the team known as disciples! The breakthrough of God was theirs to embrace.

The divestiture of privilege began with the one who had none and is the ground of hope, for those whose lives the economy has made hopeless. What Reiger calls "stunning discrepancies" (p. 42) is not only the place to begin imagining a relationship of religion and economy but where an "irruption" is most likely; actually, the only place! Jürgen Moltmann, shaped by marginalization in the holocaust affirms, "those who hope in Christ can no longer put up with reality as it is, but begin to suffer under it, to contradict it. Peace with God means conflict with the world, for the goad of the promised future stabs inexorably into the flesh of every unfulfilled present!"(*The Theology of Hope*, p. 21). The poor and those in solidarity with them trigger an irruption that subverts the permanence of the market economy. That is theology from below and it calls for economics from below. When we begin with the excluded and "that God is among them", there is a map that leads to de-absolutizing the market. Consider this: in the midst of all the limitations and ambiguities "we can build not the Kingdom of God, but societies and institutions, that in spite of all ambiguities and limitations, in being more just and brotherly and sisterly ones, may also be anticipatory signs of the definitive Kingdom" (Sung, p. 99). That may be a modest beginning but it inaugurates a definitive ending! But what might some of those "anticipatory signs" be? What might it look like to "put on the whole armor of God"? (Eph 6:11). How might one begin to live in the truth that the reign of God subverts the reign of Wall Street? "Occupy Wall Street" may not be the answer but it does center the question. And it grasps that the economy can make privilege permanent, or provisionally so.

At the very heart of "Occupy Wall Street" was a movement of common people centered on what they as a community had in common. "We are the 99 percent" is an arresting slogan but it implies the priority of community over individuals. It has been forgotten that "We the people" was once subversive! And that sets privilege "on notice". While democratic capitalism celebrates the individual and a system rigged to personal achievement, signs of the Kingdom affirm the interrelatedness of all and responsibility for one another. By contrast, the economy celebrates the authorization of individual self-enactment. A sign of a coming Kingdom is one in which community has priority and the individual flourishes in the mix. Existence is organic not autonomous.

Perhaps enough has been said to stress the prominence of the individual as autonomous decision-makers; the burden to self-construction and "entrepreneurial energy" as the center piece of morality. Daniel M. Bell Jr. calls attention to the claims that: "For Smith the dominant forces in human life were 'the uniform, constant and uninterrupted effort of every man to better his own condition...'" (p. 100). Strident self-love fashions finally the benefit of all, so we are told. By contrast to the mobilizing individualism, the alternative is the individual in community. We are who we are in relationships and in responsibility to each other for the condition of human flourishing. The Body of Christ is more than a slogan pointing toward the church. It is the recognition that "if one member suffers all suffer with it... and if one member is honored, all rejoice together with it" (I Cor 12:26). We are "constituted by our relationships" and "owe everything to others" (Reiger and Pui-Lan, p. 64). Some scholars call attention to the doctrine of the Trinity as a manifestation of relationality. While each is identifiable it is grounded in commonality. There is a representation of unity in difference. And we are called to be in the "image of God". Then the agenda is solidarity not solitude and singularity. The grip of the economy is threatened.

The individual in community is an "anticipatory sign" which has repercussions for private property. While the economy idolizes wealth and sees the accumulation of it as an obligation, within the Christian tradition it is desacralized. It subverts the dogma, "I own therefore I am". Possessing possessions can be a condition of survival but it is rendered relative by relationality. The centrality of eating, housing, clothing, health are the forms of our responsibility to and for one another. Sung states it starkly when he writes, "Salvation comes through the pursuit of eating, drinking, clothing, housing, health, freedom, affection and acceptance for the little ones, for those excluded by society, those who cannot pay us back or reciprocate" (p. 10); "good news to the poor" (Luke 4:18) is not a sentiment but a sanctuary where our relationship with God is constituted. And the consequences of that are bold in the blunt reality we have a debt to the poor, the gifting of what is rightfully theirs. Moe-Lobeda quotes Ambrose in the fourth century who wrote: "You are not making a gift of your possessions to the poor person you are handing over to him what belongs to him." And then Thomas Aquinas: "the superfluous goods that a few persons possess belong by natural right to the sustenance of the poor" (p. 209). To live in that understanding of possessions is certainly an "anticipatory sign" which resists the individualism generated by the market economy.

Yet another "anticipatory sign" that has been previously stroked but deserves further attention is the centrality of power in the market economy and the contours of powerlessness in Christianity. In reality money and power are connected. Likely this is what Stephen Colbert coined in the phrase "money theism". While commonly thought of as purchasing power, and it is that, the larger truth is that money has "agency". It has "social power, a power that shapes everything... money increasingly creates its own reality" (Joerg Reiger, p. 78). And the fact is it becomes a "player" (p. 78) which establishes the environment and condition within which we live. To join theism and money is to solidify the power evident in money and those who have it. It is one thing to say "money talks", it is more compelling to say "money acts". Economists may want to think of money as a means of exchange; it is that. More importantly it is an instrument of action. Again, "it creates its own reality" and while one can designate it as a human construct it functions as the reality in which humans and their communities live. Again "money acts" in that it has the power to construct a world in which mortals exist. And it is one in which human flourishing is diminished. Those with money can make things happen – and can prevent things from happening! Those without it have no vote! As a "theism" it ensures that nothing about the economy is provisional. It establishes that "tomorrow has been cancelled". In other terms, wealth is sacralized; then things cannot be different, or so it is claimed.

This consideration of the power of money leads us to call out an earlier theme: "the power of the powerless". That cuts in two directions. First, when the poor, marginalized, and oppressed name their condition, the prospects of revolt and rebellion emerge. The seeds of hope take on possibilities among those who have nothing to lose and everything to gain. The desire that fuels the market is subverted into a desire for human flourishing and fulfillment. The future arises from those who have none. A community of the forsaken gathers "eschatological energy" that rises up to meet powers which are reconceived as provisional. It is no surprise that in history whenever there is radical change it is from below; power from above may prevail for a time but the gathering of the "nonperson" in multiple forms leads to an "irruption". But, second, that irruption is also undergirded by the God present in "the poor Christ". Rieger again reminds us that "God chooses what is foolish in the world to shame the wise; God chooses what is weak in the world to shame the strong; God chose what is low and despised in the world... to reduce to nothing things that are" (I Corinthians 1:27-28). It is strictly bottom-up that claims and defines the future. The "self-emptying of God" transpired in a "construction worker... [and] that turns things upside down" (Reiger, p. 129). The suffering God stands with and stands against, and that renders provisional at best everything that claims to be permanent. The market economy is a human construct; the reign of God is a divine one. God is at work in the poor and therein resides the ultimate "power of the powerless".

Conclusion

In summation, the articulation of a fourth position on economy and religion has been more circular than linear. Central to the argument is the premise that the economy has become a religion. It is the stark reality as one seeks to liberate privilege in the matrix of economics and religion. There the market functions as an ultimate that transcends ambiguities and creates a sense of permanence. Rituals, creeds, worship, and coalesce to preempt a sense of being provisional. And desire is prominent in the process. But there are "anticipatory signs" which erode – perhaps modestly initially – the sanctuary of privilege. To assert that privilege enthrones straight, white, males is only to underscore the obvious. It would be an overreach to claim the market economy is teetering on the brink of collapse; or perhaps should be. But there are some forms of resistance, "anticipatory signs", which subvert the *status quo* and do so as a legacy of a religious heritage. There exists a tension between the economy and religion. The "poor Christ" resists the economy's addiction to wealth. The primacy of community in the faith tradition erodes the individuals generated by the market. And "the power of the powerless" neuters the primacy of wealth.

Occupy Religion fashions the argument in the verbiage of

immanence and transcendence, things "that belong to the world –and things that go beyond it" (p. 71). The issues form around a transcendence that gets domesticated and an immanence that gets celebrated beyond its merit. This diminishing of privilege involves keeping transcendence open and immanence less than a dwelling place (p. 78). Under the best of circumstances the dialectic of immanence and transcendence leads to "the new world... growing in the midst of the old" (p. 76). Then straight, white, males can preempt the privilege and join in the human process of flourishing. Then liberation becomes an agenda and the breakthrough of God sustains it.

Bibliography

Berger, Peter (Editor) *The Capitalist Spirit*. (San Francisco: ICS Press, 1990).

Bowler, Kate, *Blessed*. (New York: Oxford University Press, 2013).

Douglas, Kelly Brown, *Black Bodies and The Black Church*. (New York: Palgrave MacMillan, 2013).

Gutierrez, Gustavo, *The Density of the Present*. (Maryknoll: Orbis Books, 2004).

The God of Life. (Maryknoll: Orbis Books, 1991).

The Power of the Poor in History. (Maryknoll: Orbis Books, 1983).

The Truth Shall Make You Free. (Maryknoll: Orbis Books, 1990).

Mitchem, Stephanie Y, *Name It and Claim It*. (Cleveland: The Pilgrim Press, 2007).

Moe-Lobeda, Cynthia, *Resisting Structural Evil*. (Minneapolis: Fortress Press, 2013).

Moltmann, Jürgen, *The Theology of Hope*. (New York: Harper and Row, 1967).

Nelson, Robert H., *Economics as Religion*. (Pennsylvania: Pennsylvania State University Press, 2001).

Novak, Michael, *The Spirit of Democratic Capitalism*. (New York: Madison Books, 1982).

Rieger, Joerg, *No Rising Tide*. (Minneapolis: Fortress Press, 2009).

Rieger, Joerg and Pui-lan, Kwok, *Occupy Religion*. (New York: Rowman and Littlefield
Publishers, 2012).

Sung, Jung Mo, *Desire, Markets, and Religion*. (London: SCM Press, 1988).

Chapter Four

Piety, Patriotism, and Privilege

As some face the altar in a sanctuary they may be distressed that the American flag is prominently positioned on one side and another flag with religious symbols on the other, apparently verifying the one on the opposite side of the altar. The triangulation of flags and altar appears to them as a hint that ultimacy is evenly distributed. Other worshipers may hold fast to the creed, "This nation under God", and be confident a Transcendent dimension is secured appropriately. No authorization intended. Confidence prevails in one and distress in the other; patriotism and piety protrude and for some a call for differentiation. And privilege is lurking behind it. Many may be comfortable singing "God Bless America" in church while others remember the blending of the swastika and the cross in another era. The worry is that God becomes domesticated. A lively conversation on the flag may be worth having but a movement for its withdrawal could be unproductive at best.

At issue, of course, is not the flag; location is. Interestingly some are not so sure. One form of dispute has emerged in our Capitol. An amendment to the Constitution has been crafted which speaks to the "physical desecration of the flag" and one of its proponents suggests "alone of all flags, it has the sanctity of revelation". But another Congress person protests "our flag, while revered, is a secular symbol and thus should not be worshipped" (Robert Jewett, *Mission and Menace*, pp. 283-284). The flag is for saluting, period. Nothing sacred is entailed. There is always, or potentially, power in symbols and what they designate should be under consideration. The concern is that piety will become a subset of patriotism. Over time traditional straight, white, males have been proficient at that! And privilege aspires to sacred authorization.

I

It might be more fruitful to explore the concerns in a framework less contentious. In the measure one wants to sort out the issues central to patriotism and piety, a set of contemporary narratives might be explored: what is the difference between the ways in which they are blended in the rhetoric of Martin Luther King and the ways in which they were in the events surrounding 9/11? In both, piety and patriotism are in contention or collusion. Their interface is prominent and convincing to some – and not others. Each set of narratives provides considerable allegiance and prophetic disposition. In at least some discourse, neither one is menaced by humility! Piety is prominent in a political (patriotic) agenda. Privilege is prominent in both.

Martin Luther King Jr. was, of course, a preacher and his involving of religious language is predictable; the political implications of it less so perhaps. The most obvious and compelling rhetoric of King drew confident connections between the deliverance of the Israelites and the civil rights movement. He notes that both the oppressed Israelites and the oppressed Black community were enabled to envision a "Promised Land" and be confident God would "be ahead of them in the clouds" and there was an indisputable overlap. Along the way he counseled protestors to have their activities carried out "with dignity and Christian love". The non-violence he inherited from Gandhi he was confident was authorized by the New Testament. At the conclusion of the bus boycott against discrimination he equated "reconciliation" with "redemption". And at the Washington movement his "I have a dream" speech was infused with biblical allusions. He anticipated he might not make it "to the Promised Land" but affirmed that this journey for justice would be assured by the God of justice. In every sense his piety underwrote a political agenda. And the flag was prominent as well, if only for security.

Certainly the events of 9/11 could yield a purely secular agenda. While there may be an element of that in the narrative crafted by President George W. Bush, the fusion of piety and patriotism prevailed in his role as "preacher-in-chief". He personified the historic contributions of straight, white, males. Often as not the shock of 9/11 hovers around the reality we were invaded in a sense for the first time in history. Our wars and our global struggles were transactions on the real estate of others. But the more relevant issue might be the sense in which America had assumed some sacred overtones. It was allegedly on the ship coming over that Governor Winthrop invoked "the city on a hill" image and the trail as this often translated into indications of being a "chosen people" undergirded by Transcendent attachments. Some would see both images as thefts from the biblical tradition.

It is possible but somewhat difficult to separate the event of 9/11 from the rhetoric in which President Bush framed them. President Bush under the tutelage of Billy Graham had a profound sense of God's direction in his personal life which he frequently transposed into a national agenda. He repeatedly affirmed "How good we are" and that an "axis of evil" was at large in the opposition. He was not hesitant to claim the existence of "a wonder working power" active in our national life. And he was bold to claim "we have a calling from beyond the stars to stand for freedom..." In one of his more ubiquitous affirmations he declared "God wanted me to bomb Iraq". In robust rhetoric and with a confident narrative, President Bush stepped forward to establish a fusion between the God of the Bible and American foreign policy.

Both King and Bush unambiguously blend their agendas with a version of the biblical faith. Both claim a breakthrough of God. Is there any difference between the two? In a sense, both build bridges between events at hand and those of the biblical era. Rightly so; a God of history is not locked in the past or framed in the heavens. But, can one claim legitimate mirroring in both proclamations? Are there "prisms that refract the history and cultural norms of early Israel for a twenty-first century audience" (Hugh R.Page Jr., *Israel's Poetry of Resistance*, p. IX)? When Bush and King are moving between "this and that" are the bridges touching comparable realities? Are the transactions comparable? Is the Spirit energizing resistance or is a self-interested agenda protruding?

It is certainly clear, as we have argued previously, that the Scriptural events are driven from below, from those marginalized and bereft of clear options. Whether it is the Israelites or events centering on Jesus and those who followed him, the reality of oppression predominates. And God is, as James Cone argues, the God of the oppressed who suffers with them and toward a new future. The Scriptures are not about the privileged, except insofar as they are on the wrong side of history. And they are not alone. This suggests that the bridge King provides is between "a then and a now" with striking resemblances. The only privilege is the God who sides with them. One need not critique the personal religiosity of President Bush to examine his 9/11 rhetoric. "It is what it is" and it need not provoke dismissal. But the transition from personal to public piety is another move that begs for examination. While it is likely that America was victimized, clearly the persons and structures on this scene were. One need not dispute that God has an agenda for America to envision similarities between the Israelites and the tragic events of 9/11 inappropriate at best and disingenuous at worst. What exists on either side of the bridge bears no resemblance to each other. The most powerful nation in the world clearly experiences tragic circumstances but oppression and marginalization were not among them. We were still "the land of the free and the home of the brave", at least with tarnished self-image. And the "God of our Fathers", political fathers, bore slight resemblances to the One whom Jesus called Father. That Parent put privilege at risk.

Whether or not one is distressed by the flag alongside the altar, using religion to sustain our patriotism is beyond defense. And in the measure piety is at the service of that to which the flag points, the faith tradition has been compromised and polluted. C. Eric Lincoln labeled it "Americanity."

II

That piety and patriotism are intuitively linked to power may not initially evoke recognition. Aggressive debates likely would not center on the premise both are necessary, even inevitable. But controversy arises around the degree to which one or the other or both are benign and innocent. However, less than radical unmasking should reveal that power resides in the sacred and the political in bold ways. The love of country and the love of God are instances of power for those who profess them. Whether they are perceived or collateral realities, mired in tensions, or one collapsed into the other any challenging by true believers provokes elevated blood pressure.

To submit the issues to deeper analysis might not lead to an evaluation of events leading up to the decision for crucifixion. But the drama of Jesus and Pilate is worthy of analysis, perhaps even introspection. An entrenched tradition has a power structure hierarchical in nature. Pilate has Jesus under surveil-lance and presumptively at his discretion. The best spin would seem to designate the encounter as the power resident in Pilate and the truth embodied in Jesus. Clearly Pilate has "a network of influence and leverage" (Walter Brueggemann, *Truth Speaks to Power*, p. 2). And typically, Pilate seeks "out versions of truth that are compatible with present power arrangements" (p. 4). Curiously, Pilate attempted to preempt the exercise of power; "I find no crime in him" (John 18:38). And he held out an alternative; the crowd did not prefer Barabbas, a robber (John18:4). Pilate then reposed his jurisdiction and he "took Jesus and scourged him": he imposed a crown of thorns and the symbolic purple robe. Once more Pilate attempted to "opt out" and lay it out to the crowd with the instruction "take him yourselves and crucify him" (19:6). They were ready even as Pilate was reluctant. At best, he was a victim of location.

At that point Pilate re-engages Jesus who gave no answer to a relatively benign question. "Do you not know I have the power to release you and the power to crucify you?" Then Jesus submits his claim: "You would have no power over me unless it is given from above...." (John 19:11). At that point the drama gets inverted. As Paul Lehmann asserts, now it is *Pilate before Jesus*! (*The Transfiguration of Politics*, pp. 48-70). The agent of the state is suddenly at risk. Power itself is called into question and the silence of Jesus and his later retort submit "validation". Lehmann goes on to clarify: "the point and purpose of the presence of Jesus *in the world*, and now before Pilate, are to bear witness to the truth, that is, to make effective room for the reality of God over against the world...." (p. 53). And Lehmann notes, the "calm and confident Jesus"... [trumps] an uneasy and tormented Pilate" (p. 59). The power of the state and the power of God are joined. Ironically the silence of Jesus uncorks the jurisdiction of Pilate. "The silence of Jesus is the sign that the end is the beginning of a new humanizing order of affairs" (p 66). By any measure, Jesus is unpatriotic; the piety of "time and space" for God unmasks power and renders it harmless. Jesus preempts differences and invokes God. Brueggemann notes that the narrative echoes the Exodus, certainly in a community of memory (p. 12). Jews at the time could not have heard it otherwise. It was a defining moment with prophetic validation prominent. The breakthrough of God is embodied.

And that word calls for a reconfiguration of power in its manifestation as powerlessness! Think of the event allegedly at the inception of Jesus' ministry. When Solomon conceived of and executed the building of the temple in Jerusalem it was an unambiguous assertion that God has been captured for political advantage. It kept God in "his" place, authorizing the regime of the King. What could be more audacious and presumptuous than for an unknown Jew to stand up and read from the book of Isaiah: "the Spirit of the Lord is upon me, because he has anointed me to preach good news to the poor. He has sent me to proclaim release to the captives and the recovery of sight to the blind, and to set at liberty those who are oppressed, to proclaim the acceptable year of the Lord" (Luke 4:18). Those are prerogatives appropriate to a king. Is he delusional? Or is the power of weakness forthcoming? Lehmann again alleges that "the power of weakness, when borne by a messianic presence, is the disclosure in weakness of a strength that turns, as it were, the flank of strength that has been unmasked as weakness" (p. 33). And that makes a world of differences without worldly power! It seems a new beginning and the end of worldly power and a "counter imagination" is released in the world. And it is a strange new world in which Pilate and the state are at the mercy of Jesus and the faith community. In the end it is the Easter narrative that triggers the vulnerability of the powerful. Piety subverts patriotism in the unmasking of power. In Pilate before Jesus power is unmasked and neutered, and the final validation is an empty tomb. While Pilate can orchestrate execution he cannot thwart the weakness that overwhelms it. The power to refuse power in silence is vindicated, leaving Pilate no place to go for vindication. In thwarting the authority of Pilate, patriotism has yielded to piety. And power has become limp! Piety on the cross subverts privilege and signals an impending breakthrough.

III

While one may be conversant with the claims of American exceptionalism, a religious framework is not necessary or inevitable. Patriotism may prevail without concurrent piety. In an era marked by secularism, a severance is apt to prevail or at least be preferred.

Exceptionalism can be understood as a communal act of self-authorization and appraisal. One scholar writes of a "missionary persuasion" with a new insistence that America be admired, almost worshipped (Godfrey Hodgson, *The Myth of American Exceptionalism*, p. XII). While the rest of the world may have a deficit of confidence, arrogance elevates the nation into a hubristic existence that eventually takes the form of invulnerability. Its capacity for self-congratulation places the nation beyond the contours of nationalism. Certainly the founding fathers had a hand in the formation of a Constitution and the Declaration of Independence. While not entirely original, they were gifted with a disposition to identify the nation with the highest ideals and structures in history. It was a version of liberation, albeit a delusional one.

Confirmation of that exceptionalism was enhanced by "the disintegration of communism" first evident in the collapse of the Berlin Wall, and in the emergence of the lone superpower status confirming that none were like us. And the duplicitous feature is a sense of uncontested eminence. "Only partly in jest, President George W. Bush saw himself as the world's sheriff" (p. 28). And any estimate of a sheriff is marked by a curious mix of power and perversity. While espousing the mobility of democracy, "It replaced the divine right, and hereditary right, and customary legitimacy with this supreme authority of the people" (p. 36). One has only to reflect on the era of the cold war to find evidence of unmatched superiority. The world's geography was transformed and the "military-industrial complex" was sufficient to establish victory, power, and prominence in world affairs. Plenty and power coalesced to reassure one's prominence in global affairs. Privilege reigns! That it would find expression in foreign policy was a given and a gift to world order.

A former Secretary of State referred to America as "the indispensable nation" (Madeline Albright, *The Mighty and the Almighty*, pp. 31-32). As such it has a responsibility for world governance. Apparently one does not have to think like a straight, white, male! But the exercise of power is not a function of strength alone but its innocence and purity. As such it is totally appropriate to position oneself as a model for others, and if need be execute it. Exceptionalism has a passport to privilege. While this mentality may currently be particularly intense, it has an origin often alluded to by Presidents like Reagan, Johnson, and Bush. They reference a sermon by John Winthrop on the journey to a new land: "we shall be as a city upon a hill, the eyes of all people are upon us" (quoted in Conrad Cherry, *God's New Israel*, pp. 42-43). The trail of that leads to further biblical lineages: we are "God's chosen people", and "the new Israel". As such we are on a mission, a global one free of boundaries. The interests of all are served by the grandeur of our reality, graciously shared (or imposed!). One administrator in particular conceived of the Iraq war as evidence of global benevolence (Woodyard, *The Church in the Time of Empire*, pp. 14-17).

But then there was 9/11! Exceptionalism experienced a facelift, or perhaps a tummy tuck. Vulnerability was in evidence, an essentially new experience for Americans. The presumption prevailed that the land was secure, beyond the reach of alien forces. The closest threat was Pearl Harbor and that seemed more on ships than space. Reinhold Niebuhr wrote prophetically that the "false security to which all men are tempted is the security of power" (*Beyond Tragedy*, p. 98). The pillars of a righteous and mighty society were rendered insufficient against the intentions of a few "traitors". As the sole superpower surely no nation would dare. But a handful of individuals did and the myth of a sacred space was torpedoed. Power no longer assured invulnerability after 9/11. The damage to the national psyche was astronomical. In a sense the American soul was terrorized at the Twin Towers, the World Trade Center, the Pentagon, and presumptively the Capitol itself. President Bush reading a children's story in Texas and Vice President Cheney in the basement of the White House were not able to restore the illusion of exceptionalism. Some wounds are not subject to erasure.

President Bush with his arms around a firefighter and a megaphone to amplify his considerable voice could not resurrect exceptionalism. For once power was helpless and authority was problematic. Movements to grieve and then move on could not heal the wounds to exceptionalism and the confidence in power and the illusion of innocence. For the moment at least it had suffered a mortal blow and resurrection seemed unlikely. Those with a religious spin tried. Some scholars with reputations for judicious engagement were blunt in the assault on claims of innocent victimization. The efforts to repair or restore the American soul were dismissed with the claim "the official account of 9/11 is false and this false account has been used to support this farther extension of the American Empire" (David Ray Griffin & Peter Dale Scott Eds., *9/11 and American Empire*, p. VIII). Duplicitous portrayals were devastated and then dismissed by allegations of "conspiring theorists". Without engaging the debate, one can name efforts to purify the sacrifice. Judicious author and journalist, Anna Quindlen exonerated a mediation on 9/11 by Eugene Kennedy. Likely he was on the mark with the assertion, "the headlines in that Tuesday's morning papers are the last pictures we have of a world unaware it would never be the same again" (*9/11 Meditations at the Center of the World*, p. 5). But then the rhetoric shifts: "we embrace the city where God is surely present to us in the smoking ruins from whose sight we can fashion no distraction" (p. 29). Sacred space has been violated. But perhaps the claims of exceptionalism are mixed with ashes. Piety can hardly resurrect the politics and patriotism.

While the setting of exceptionalism has largely been secured in the secular framework, it is not likely to rest there. The reality, as has been suggested previously, is that a sacred dimension of exceptionalism readily gains prominence. This is most common when the nation has a President with a vivid religious experience. As noted earlier, President Bush has been identified by some as "preacher-in-chief". The swiftest evidence of that is the claim "God wanted me to bomb Iraq" and similar sacralization of a national agenda. While this may have peaked in the Bush presidency, it is not uniquely situated there. One can call up a vivid American Civil Religion as is evident in the work of Robert Bellah. But piety can be more conspicuously sacred. Exceptionalism is reluctantly a "stand alone" phenomenon. It thirsts for ultimate authorization and legitimacy. The nation under God is more likely this God under the nation. One could argue that exceptionalism and the sacred became synonymous. Just the truth mentioned earlier, *The Mighty and the Almighty*, would appear to situate God under the "jurisdiction of nationalism". Piety and patriotism/political are in sync, congenial, and comfortably aligned. Privilege preservers! Up to this point, straight, white, males have been on the wrong side of history, the history God unfolds and a new world evolves.

IV

Piety at its best can expose the demons in patriotism. Consider Jeremiah Wright. The media got it wrong. Their "unsolicited interjection" (John L. Jackson in *The Obama Phenomenon* p. 165) severed content from context; location and message are cohorts, even combatants. In the framework of the Black Church, a bulwark for grief and resistance, "goddamn American" had legitimate echoes, even necessary ones. In the spirit of the biblical prophets the pastor "called out" the nation in the name of justice. Historically the Black Church has been a place for sharing wounds inflicted by white supremacy: "nobody knows the trouble I've seen…" rings true and echoes through the memory and the reality of being black in America. But it is also an agent of resistance and even revolt. Consider all the ministers surrounding the Reverend Martin Luther King, Black and White to be sure, and the defiance of honky norms. Militancy shaped by love and in the form of justice is a bulwark. While "courteous accommodation" has often shaped the public images, it cannot finally obscure "Black religion's confrontational prophetic tradition" (p. 167). Resistance to slavery was the wound of the Black Church's creation. In the light of that Jeremiah Wright is simply engaged in a "symbolic reversal," is exposing the demons in patriotism. As such it is disingenuous and perverse to designate him an "agitator" (p. 197).

Consider a portion of the sermon entitled "Confusing God and Government" as a framework from which the press engaged in an excision:

Not God Bless America, God damn America. That's in the Bible, killing innocent people. God damn America for treating her citizens as less than human. God damn America for as long as she acts like she is God and she is supreme. The United States government failed the vast majority of her citizens of African descent.

And "while whites sought to communicate with an essentially private African American religious audience" (p. 171) the prophetic imagination "outed" public sins violating international justice. And the Black community understood because they were of a piece with their own almost 400 years in a white society. In these words the "symbolic reversal" circled the centuries and eventually went global.

…when it comes to treating her citizens of Indian descent fairly, she failed. She put them on reservations. When it came to treating her citizens of Japanese descent, she failed. She put them in internment camps. When it came to treating her citizens of African descent fairly, America failed. The government put them in chains. She put them in slave quarters, put them on auction blocks, put them in cotton fields, put them in inferior schools, put them in substandard housing, put them in scientific experiments, put them in the lowest paying jobs, put them outside the protection of the law, kept them out of their racist bastions of higher education, and locked them into positions of hopelessness and helplessness. The government gives them drugs, builds bigger prisons, passes a three strike law and then wants them to sing God Bless America.

It is worth remembering that Barack Obama did not bring any religiosity to the table when he, as a young lawyer, advocated for justice in the south side of Chicago. Initially his journey of hope for a different world preempted balanced theology with ecclesial moorings. But in time he learned of a church and a pastor whose agenda matched his own, indeed undergirded it. His spirituality was born in the streets as he found an institution with an agenda imbedded in its DNA. It is not difficult to imagine him fired by the rhetoric of Jeremiah Wright. Here was a preacher and pastor, versed generously in the theology of James Cone, who framed his agenda in transcendent terms. They were about what he was about with an authority only transcendence can critique. His was a piety in the service of patriotism uncommon in the churches and unimaginable on the streets. But it was there, even as evil was. The piety prevailed against the ways of the world. Here public discourses prevailed against forms of patriotism which preempted its origins and indeed rebuked them. The prophets of old came alive in the preaching the media prompted white America to reject. The castration of privilege is not good "news" in a controlled media.

Initially Barack Obama got it right when he confided he could no more sever his commitment to Jeremiah Wright than disown a member of his family. Perhaps understandably as a candidate for President the baggage was more than he could handle. But you have to wonder if rejection of his pastor felt like an irreverent compromise. For the reality is that this subverts the biblical tradition evident in the prophets. The penetration of patriotism and the exposure of idolatry linked to perversity are normative. Piety has to turn to patriotism when it turns from the God of justice. Public discourse on the role of the church and its faith tradition controls the worldly formation of our justice in the sanctuary as well as the streets. The church is called to be the enemy of the state when the state is at odds with the purposes of God. Calling out the perversity of patriotism from the halls of piety is a sacred duty embodied in the biblical prophets. Consider Amos: "Let justice fall down like waters, and righteousness like an overflowing stream" (Amos 6:24). And then play the words of Jeremiah Wright against the ruminations of Fox News:

> We took the country by terror, away from the Sioux, the Apache, the Arawak, the Comanche, the Arapahoe, the Navajo. We bombed Granada and killed innocent citizens.... We bombed the black Cuban community of Panama with Stealth bombers and killed unarmed teenagers, toddlers, pregnant mothers and hardworking fathers... we bombed a plant in Sudan to pay back for the attack on our embassy... we bombed Hiroshima, we bombed Nagasaki. America chickens are coming home to roost.

How can one suppress the echoes of biblical prophets too long caged in sanctuaries of irrelevance and accomodatory patriotism? Jeremiah Wright facing off white supremacy in the government, the military and the media is but a reflection of Helmut Thielicke in a Tubingen church preaching for justice while the gestapo soldiers lined the sanctuary around with machine guns. Hardly a voice in the wilderness or a whisper in the streets! It is piety impregnated with a prophetic tradition which renders patriotism an honorable tradition which has been raped by self-serving national agendas.

Intuitively Jeremiah Wright knew, perhaps with a spin from James Cone, that Jesus was anything but patriotic. His piety had better things to structure with his agenda. The temple was sacred- secular territory, ruled and run by the political establishment, and Jesus had the audacity to announce its demise. And he even bordered on violence in relation to the money changers there. Any patriotic person would know there was a sacred settlement about the clean and unclean; and he had the audacity to dismiss it. It was less than cool to win over the tax collector who was an agent and emissary of the regime. Healing on the Sabbath was conspicuously unpatriotic as it was "the law of the land" and to violate it was not a sacred but a secular defilement. At every point he made common cause with the marginals and made them principles in the kingdom of God. Of course, the cross was a reward for his lack of patriotism! In more ways than one can recall Jesus effectively said "God damn the state". Jeremiah Wright was only mimicking his savior on that day in the pulpit of the United Church of Christ. The Jesus event echoed through the sermon. And it did not serve the purposes of a candidate for President of the United States.

But the preacher and sermon do not stand alone in Black worship. Piety can carry a tune alien to the interest of patriotism. While the idiom of rap, hip hop, and spirituals are starker and perhaps subversive, the more evidently benign gospel and blues music when decoded are offensive even threatening. Ironically, sung by color blended choirs, usually tilting to white, seem safe and even entertaining while subliminally advance the interests of liberation. Once decoded their offense to patriotism is on display and provides rhythmic support for the preacher's message. Subversion is not inevitably signaled in blatant terms of rebellion. But what precedes that is the development of a consciousness and an identity which can resist. Then David L. Moody writes, referencing W.E.B. Du Bois, "as an interpreter of the spirituals, Du Bois conveys to his audience the importance of the Negro Spiritual in the formation of a consciousness. When confronted with dehumanizing situations, it was the spirit-filled melodies of 'these songs' that kept the mind and the body of the African American together" (*Political Melodies in the Pews* p. 10). Music had the function of giving expression to hope against despair and joy against death itself. The word of the preacher alone was not sufficient to sustain integration and identity. Singing was and is a centering activity which enables survival and expectation. "Personal agency" is sustained and empowered for African Americans through "Sorrow Songs" (p. 13) as the forces of white supremacy close in and disable. But the "coded message" might seem benign to the oppressor: "crossing over Jordan" was "a reference to escaping to the northern side of the Ohio River by means of the Underground Railroad… [it] was a network of people who hid fugitive slaves and helped them escape to freedom…" (p. 14). Piety turned political undermined patriotism. And the white slave owners, and their original acts of supremacy, never "got the message" of subversion of their interests. The spoken word of revolt was put to music in ways apparently benign. Hence the bond between God and an oppressed people was both preached Word and vibrant melody.

When Jeremiah Wright engaged in "symbolic reversal" the choir and the congregation were set on a journey of liberation. Piety gored patriotism and blood spilled inevitably. To his credit, Barack Obama in *The Audacity of Hope*, acknowledged in reference to Wright's claim, "I was drawn to the power of the African American religious tradition to spur social change" (quoted in Moody p 39). One has to wonder how much of that echoed in the White House. Piety's intervention in patriotism calls for a liberating community. "Yet to understand and appreciate fully Reverend Wright and President Obama, one must also develop a sophisticated appreciation for the complexity of black religion" (Jackson, p. 177).

Afterword

The journey with piety and patriotism calls for a final test. What would be revealed if it was laid beneath the cross and concurrent events? Hovering around the crucifixion narrative is not a comfortable place to be: the suffering God is in full display and the orders of the world are embraced by evil. But being there may yield a voice we have not heard. One that sets privilege on edge.

The disciples were with Jesus when it was safer – in the upper room with a sacrament in the making. Even Judas was among them. The next day Jesus was alone, essentially without acts of compassion until one person embraced the burden of the cross. Even the women, typically more faithful, viewed the events from afar – or so it was reported, they "stood at a distance". Carrying the cross is difficult enough to imagine but being on it beyond comprehension. A shiny brass or gold cross on the altar is so much more compatible with our sensitivities. Some brutal acts followed with only one gesture of compassion. Those gathered "mocked him" (Matthew 27:31). Then, "he saved others; he cannot save himself" (Matthew 27:42). All the signs were that he was finished. But of course he wasn't; Easter morning was forthcoming. Now when it was over that day, patriotism hit the mark while piety was on the run. It was a centurion, one of the "military industrial complex," who put it right: "Truly this was a son of God" (Luke 23:54). And others acknowledged he was innocent (Luke 23:54).

What could be more unlikely than that patriotism spoke when piety had abandoned Jesus? Odd, is it not; a soldier decoded the event and declared what piety overlooked; what might one draw from that? Perhaps the truth attested finally in Scripture does not always reside in the self-evidently faithful. God may provoke the world to express the Word! If not regularly, at least in moments. And that sets us to look and listen in unlikely places for the Words God speaks outside the orbit of faith. Even the patriotic voice can speak a discerning word in events bleak for the moment. How odd of God to choose a soldier while aspiring saints were on the run! "Truly..." an agent of patriotism proclaimed the Word.

One emerging scholar powerfully concludes this narrative with the following commentary:

This soldier was the first to proclaim the consequences of Jesus' death, but he is not the last. The story continues, for the crucified One rose from the dead and calls each of us to attest to the efficacy of his death through our words, our actions, and the affliction and liberation that flow into our lives. As we heed the call, we take our place next to a Roman centurion.... (Nathaniel D. Hieb, *Christ Crucified in a Suffering World*, p 244)

"Next to a Roman centurion"? How uncomfortable would that be? Unless, of course, the centurion for the moment is the straight, white, male we are meant to be. And the breakthrough of God is on the cusp.

Bibliography

Albright, Madeline. *The Mighty and the Almighty*. (New York, Harper Perennial, 2006).

Bacevich, Andrew J. *The Limits of Power*. (New York, Henry Holt and Company, 2008).

Brueggemann, Walter. *Truth Speaks to Power*. (Louisville, Westminster John Knox Press, 2013).

Cherry, Conrad (ed). *God's New Israel*. (Englewood Cliffs, Prentice-Hall, 1971).

Griffin, David Ray, and Scott, Peter Dale (eds). *9/11 and American Empire*. (Northhampton, Olive Branch Press, 2007).

Griffin, David Ray. *The Christian Faith and the Truth Behind 9/11*. (Louisville, Westminster John Knox Press, 2006).

Hieb, Nathan D. *Christ Crucified in a Suffering World*. (Minneapolis, Fortress Press, 2013).

Hodgson, Godfrey. *The Myth of American Exceptionalism*. (New Haven, Yale University Press, 2009).

Jackson, John L. in *The Obama Phenomenon*, Henry, Charles P., Alla, Robert L., and Christmen, Robert. (Chicago, University of Illinois Press, 2009).

Jewitt, Robert. *Mission and Menace*. (Minneapolis, Fortress Press, 2008).

Kennedy, Eugene. *9/11 Meditations at the Center of the World*. (Maryknoll, Orbis Press, 2002).

Lehmann, Paul. *The Transfiguration of Politics*, (New York, Harper Row, 1975).

Moody, David L. *Political Melodies in the Pews*. (New York, Lexington Books, 2012).

Niebuhr, Reinhold. *Beyond Tragedy*. (New York, Charles Scribner's Sons, 1955).

Page, Hugh R. Jr. *Israel's Poetry of Resistance*. (Minneapolis, Fortress Press, 2013).

Wright, Jeremiah. "Sermon Excerpts" in Moody, David L., *Political Melodies in the Pews*. (New York, Lexington Books, 2012).

Woodyard, David O. *The Church in the Time of Empire*. (Washington, Circle Books, 2011).

Chapter Five

Demonic Privilege and Divine Accountability

Evidentially, Adolph Hitler was a straight, white, male perhaps one incarnating the demonic in forms we are unlikely to recognize in ourselves. With unsurpassed proficiency evil reigned in and about him in ways that challenge our imagination. While those of Jewish descent were privileged targets, blacks and homosexuals, priests and nuns among others were victims of his brutality. And a promising young Protestant theologian was hanged even as liberating troops were approaching the death camp. For many, perhaps more, the erasure of the Divine presence was accomplished in measured acts of interpersonal brutality and disingenuous acts of deceit. Michael Berenbaum argues that:

> Auschwitz represented the perverse perfection of slavery. In all previous manifestations of human slavery ...slaves were permitted to reproduce and hence to increase the master's wealth. By contrast, the Nazis reduced human beings to consumable raw materials... All mineral life was systematically drained from their bodies, which were recycled into the Nazi war economy; gold teeth went to the treasury, hair was used for mattresses, ashes became fertilizer...
>
> (*After Tragedy and Triumph* p. 24).

Many theologians, Jewish and Christian alike, would envision this as a unique setting within which to contest the involvement of the Divine in the demonic and the destiny of privilege. "Where in the world is God?" is not confined to Holocaust events but certainly framed there in compelling ways. Straight, white, males are not uniquely related to the dilemmas but their claims and methodologies are at risk. And the exposure can be unsettling at best, destructive at worst. The breakthrough of God is challenged and assessed differently.

While considering the Divine and the demonic in the Holocaust the forms of theological analysis are legion. For our purposes, one focuses on the divine commandment, Emil Fackenheim, and the other as the Divine presence, Melissa Raphael. Both struggle to make sense theologically of "what hurts". And gender is prominent in both! But not those with a same sex orientation.

I

Emil Fackenheim is, perhaps, most immediately identified with his "614th commandment." While he acknowledged that the early articulation of it was "terribly inadequate," it has qualities which are compelling and evocative, along with being unambiguous. The commandment reads: "the authentic Jew of today is forbidden to hand Hitler yet another, posthumous victory." Fackenheim goes on to explain:

> ...we are, first commanded to survive as Jews, lest the Jewish people perish. We are commanded second, to remember in our guts and bones the martyrs of the Holocaust, lest their memory perish. We are forbidden, thirdly to deny or despair of God... lest Judaism perish. We are forbidden, finally, to despair of the world, lest we help make it a meaningless place in which God is dead or irrelevant and everything is permitted.
> ("The 614th Commandment in *Holocaust: Religion: and Philosophical Implications* pp. 293-295)

If one accepts with Braiterman that "Fackenheim has said little about God" then one can understand Braiterman's conclusion that "...the poorly formulated 614th commandment..." (Zachary Braiterman, *God After Auschwitz*, p. 135) is incidental to the validity of Fackenheim's theology. It might be a foreclosure on such an enterprise! However, in addition to the compelling case to be made for giving rigorous attention to Fackenheim as a philosopher, which Braiterman has done brilliantly, Fackenheim can be read more aggressively as a theologian. Through a theological lens it is difficult to accept the conclusion that "God represents at best a minimal figure for Fackenheim" (p. 156).

Fackenheim acknowledges that "Never, within or without Jewish history, have men (likely a straight, white, male) anywhere had such dreadful, such horrifying reason for turning their backs on God" (*God's Presence in History*, p. 6). And yet, this is not where Fackenheim himself lets theology remain.

What arrests this prospect? Fackenheim appeals to what he calls "root experiences" (p. 8). These are historical and transparent while retaining an opaque quality. They are past events, which continue to negotiate reality in the present. This reality is mediated liturgically in the community of faith. It is a public event, not private. While root experiences are "natural-historical" they yield "the presence of God" (p. 10). Their proof is in their persistence in the faith community. Their reenactment has a self-authenticating quality. Astonishment, wonder, and surprise accompany them and they have an efficacy uniquely their own. A root experience is true because of what it yields, and that has only internal confirmation. A bystander would not likely be persuaded. But to the faithful Jew, the past becomes present and God is once again in the midst of the faithful. And a breakthrough is in the offering.

There are two root experiences for the Jewish people with which Fackenheim deals, and he distinguishes these carefully. The Holocaust serves as an event which separates them decisively and consequentially. One experience is that at the Sea and the other at Sinai; one embraces the "Saving Presence of God" and the other a "Commanding Presence."

There is no rapprochement between the Sinai event and the Holocaust; in the latter "God failed to save" (Braiterman, p. 141). Fackenheim writes, "...the pious Jew remembering the Exodus and the salvation at the Red Sea does not call to mind events now dead and past. He reenacts these events as a *present reality*: only thus is he assured that the past God saves still..." (*God's Presence in History*, p. 11). In Auschwitz, however, there is no "abiding astonishment" and no transparency; no meaning is yielded there.

But, while there was no saving presence in Auschwitz, there was a commanding one, and that is the other root experience. The experience at Sinai foregrounds the present and is replicated in it. There and here is one. But this is no bare bone injunction. "If the astonishment abides, it is because Divinity is *present* in the commandment" (Fackenheim, p. 152). Some argue that the 614th Commandment is a human voice; Fackenheim hears it as a Divine one. One can imagine which gender it resembles! The paradox is that the commandment both destroys and restores human freedom. Hence both terror and joy are present (p. 15-16). Lest they do Hitler's work, there Jews have a "sacred obligation to survive" (*On Jewish Life After Auschwitz*, p. 208). Through the Sinai root experience, Fackenheim preserves a Presence for the God of history, the God of Israel.

The reality of root experiences raises another issue: what Fackenheim calls "epoch making events." These are both historical and have a history. "...They are historical occasions that challenge the 'root experiences' to answer to new and often unprecedented conditions" (p. 208). While the Holocaust is the most recent epoch-making event, it has antecedents – events which were threats to the faith. Though not of the same magnitude, Fackenheim includes among these antecedents "...the destruction of the first Temple, the Maccabean revolt, the destruction of the second Temple, and the expulsion from Spain"

(*God's Presence in History*, pp 8-9). Clearly, each is a breakthrough.

Epoch-making events do not dictate a new faith but a new response from the old one. They bring forth the old one. They bring faith to a breaking point but it withstands the onslaught. They test but do not shatter. Each on its own is devastating without prevailing. Hence, while Richard Rubenstein attends services and remains silent, Fackenheim participates in the liturgy which affirms God's Presence. Some may think this is no more than a resolute habit, an addiction to a fleeting presence, but for Fackenheim the command to survive is grounded. Paul Tillich argues for keeping in play all the elements in the act of faith – will, rationality, and emotion. Fackenheim forefronts the will, but the other elements are fully present as well.

Critics like Braiterman contend that Fackenheim's God after Auschwitz is a diminished one. "God registers but a partial, fleeting presence. A trace presence, virtually absent, a still small voice, it is not quite here." Root experiences notwithstanding, "this piecemeal presence leaves history unredeemed… his vision remains comfortless" (Braiterman, p. 144). The God who once saved is now, at best, an underachiever. Perhaps "He" was not male enough!

Fackenheim's theological argument, however, largely hinges on the word "fragmentary" in relation to God's presence. Perhaps fragmentary means that something is not what it used to be. But it could be read otherwise – as something with biblical precedence. "The saving divine Presence at the Red Sea had revealed its fragmentariness, if only because the Egyptians were drowning; the divine commanding Presence at Mount Sinai had been fragmentary, if only because it could be rejected as well as accepted…" (pp. 52-54). Fackenheim seems to acknowledge that, then, as now, God's management of the household is not absolute. The Egyptians would not have drowned and the law would not have been ignored with a different mode of operation. Hence, "scandal" is an element in the divine economy. All is not accomplished in the event at hand. A fleeting presence is still there. That sounds like less than a breakthrough.

One wonders whether Fackenheim should be criticized for fragmentariness when this is in the biblical text as well. Historical events about the Divine presence are not mystical ones. Returning to his opening comments on the first Chapter of Ezekiel, Fackenheim recounts that the prophets claim that "the heavens were opened and I saw visions of God" is something from which the Hebrew Bible "shrinks... in awe and terror" (p. 3). Fragmentariness is more the norm.

The critique of Fackeinheim by Michael Wyschogrod comes from another direction. He claims that Fackenheim began with "a totally unique crime unparalleled in human history" (Michael Wyschogrod, "Faith and the Holocaust", p. 290). Since Wyschogrod sees this as a "totally destructive event" it is fatuous to presume "to extract a positive result... with the survival of the people, rather than the existence of God, as the conclusion" (p. 288). Silence is to be preferred and the resulting agenda is not to "preserve Judaism" but "to destroy Hitler" (pp. 286-289).

Is it, in fact, the case, however, that Fackenheim's point of departure is singularly the Holocaust and his goal to suck something from it? Might it not be the case that he is more nearly engaged in a method which verges on Paul Tillich's method of correlation? At one point Fackenheim appears to reject this. However, upon closer examination, it can be argued that he only rejects the form of the method when discussing the relation of philosophy and theology/religion (*Quest for Past and Future*, p. 9).

Independent of its Christian framework, the claim is that a theological system "moves back and forth between two poles, the eternal truth is its foundation and the temporal situation in which the eternal truth must be received" (Paul Tillich, *Systematic Theology*, Vol 1, p. 3). Rather than seeing the Holocaust as a point of departure, Fackenheim may be identifying it as that situation with which the "root experience" of Mt. Sinai correlates. One would not, therefore, need to dismiss "the poorly formulated 614th commandment per se" as a way of defending Fackenheim from the critique of Wyschogrod or even to reduce it to an injunction which "...constitutes God's presence in twentieth century Jewish history" as if the Voice did not have an origin in something transcendent (Braiterman p. 135, 145).

For Fackenheim, the theological project is relentlessly situational. Neither air-conditioned libraries, nor arid and musty abstractions, are its venue. And this is its most radically historical form. Fackenheim might embrace something like Tillich's method of correlation, but the situation as entrée to the eternal message, would not be one fashioned by ontological analysis. To universalize is to diminish. Fackenheim is clear that he is not concerned with man-in-general, but with one who is not only Jewish but Jewish with the Holocaust in full view. There is a there-and-then of tradition and a here-and-now of experience. The facticity of a former event is not anchored in the past; a Jew is never free of what went before. He is not only a Jew, but one who is a singled out for being Jewish (*Quest for Past and Future*, p. 16). There is "the particularly of Auschwitz," which is not continuous with essences of Jewishness but unique in history (p. 17). Yet there remains "the possibility of a religious response" (p. 18). Thus, being a Jew "here-and-now" means that the memories hold of children thrown into the flames, surgical procedures without anesthetic, extinction by gas chambers, and a final solution which was evil for evil's sake. This situation is not one that leads into the "eternal message" – it perhaps requires it, but it violates its possibility. The demonic threatens the validity of tradition rather than call out for it. And bearing witness against perpetrators is more compelling than the affirmations of the faith community.

This takes us to the reading of Scripture. Because the Holocaust forms a trauma to the faith, the Book cannot be read as it has been. Indeed, "the Jewish Bible must be read by Jews today – read, listened to, struggled with, if necessary fought against –

as though they had never read it before" (Emil L. Fackenheim, *The Jewish Bible After the Holocaust*, p. viii). The commentaries and subcommentaries of former times which mediated the continuity between the then-and-there and the here-and-now obstruct the reading of what Fackenheim calls "the naked text" (p. viii). The Holocaust creates a rupture between the reader and the text: "Jews cannot read as once they did, of God who sleeps not and slumbers not" (p. vii). Ancient forms of access to the text are now obstacles at best. This is the first generation for which "choice" was denied. To believe *a priori* is no longer an option after the Holocaust and to read as if it did not happen is the ultimate blasphemy.

It is not difficult to see why Emil Fackenheim does not remain silent in the synagogue. For him the heavens are not empty; history is a venue of the interruption of a presence. The Holocaust is a rupture that precludes a saving presence in Auschwitz. Yet, according to Fackenheim, "a Jewish believer must pause" (*God's Presence in History*, p. 6). There is a Commanding Presence, which summons the believer "to survival, to remember, not to despair of God, not to despair of the world" ("The 614th Commandment" p. 295). The consequence of this is clear with respect to ritual. Ritual is essential if we are "to mend the world." Not to engage in ritual is to preclude the possibility that "there-and-then" can become "here-and-now." As quoted above, "The pious Jew remembering the Exodus and the salvation at the Red Sea does not call to mind events now dead and gone. He enacts these events as a *present reality*: only thus is he assured that the past saving God saves still, and that He will bring ultimate salvation" (*God's Presence in History*, p. 11). The prospects of survival and remembrance, avoiding despair of God and the world, are grounded in ritual. Silence in the synagogue yields another victory for Hitler; participation yields both the presence and the promise of the God who saves. Ritual is a life-and-death matter for the authentic Jew and Fackenheim is one of them. Theology after the Holocaust is wedded to the ritual, fused at the very core of each. Typically, a white male presides!

Absent a "saving presence," a "commanding presence" is sufficient, in the preview of Fackenheim.

II

But not for Melissa Raphael. A "saving presence" may be obscured but it is also retrievable. Emil Fackenheim simply had his eye on the wrong ball and played by patriarchal rules and reality. Typically straight, white, males do! While Fackenheim does not want "to deny or despair of God", he ducks the issue of reconciling God with the Holocaust while stipulating the agenda of "the divine voice" to a version of "never again." There is no evident breakthrough of God. The commanding voice is substitution for a presence which in a sense shifts the agenda from God to the victim. Fackenheim clearly does not diminish the magnitude of evil but he is reluctant to have what others have called a "suffering God." Unable to secure a rational way to have God "there" he settles for the presence of a "voice" that commands. In a sense he does not attempt to answer "Who is God?" In reality the "voice" is disembodied! While he focuses on the reality of the Holocaust he by-passes any embodied presence. Unanswered is the question of how godly is God in the death camps. The victims are de-centered, divested of grounding. While he does not want the legacy of Hitler to win, the terms of the contest of the Divine and the demonic are unclear. How is God present as more than the "voice" is obscured? The rights of human beings trail off as the voice fades. And liberation is not a convincing agenda item.

The contrast to Melissa Raphael is stark, even startling. She crafts a book about presence and absence while acknowledging that she is part of a generation which "sees upon its flesh the scar without the wound, the memory without the direct experience"

(*The Female Face of God in Auschwitz*, p. ix). Her agenda is to hear the witnesses until their voice is blended with her own. But it is with a different ear than has been dominant in capturing the Holocaust reality. Gender has been ignored, at best she claims boldly that "women's experience of the Holocaust cannot be subsumed into that of men" (p. 1). While not to diminish the suffering of men, she aspires to a gendered analysis. Their suffering and resistance, along with that of children, must be surfaced and reflected upon. In short, she aspires to a correction not a dismissal. And this calls for a clear articulation of the very presence Fackenheim obscured. "…a female account of God's presence and absence in Auschwitz" is her agenda. And the patriarchal model of God accounts for the alleged failure of God, the divine ineptly positioned against the demonic. For Raphael men can get it right; typically they don't! Less than liberation is on the horizon.

The Nazi agenda was an erasure of God from the death camps. While acknowledging that Fackenheim can be read as "morally serious" the "commanding voice" "typifies the patriarchal refusal of the divine abjection… and it's expectation of obedience" (p. 30). And one is left with the suspicion that God was not "patriarchal enough" to avoid the suspicion of failure (p. 35). No wonder Rubenstein fell under the spell of the death of God movement. By contrast, "Religious feminism" (p. 59) celebrates the relational power-in-between persons. Echoes of Martin Buber reverberate in the claim God is right there in the midst of an I-Thou encounter. There is a "restoration of presence" (p. 42) that the Nazi regime destroyed in the dehumanized acts of the prison camp agenda. Human dignity was in every moment demolished and desecrated. Hers is a theology of image. God is present in the face, as one who does not look away, and in the measure a mortal stays in touch after the Divine has defeated the erasure of God by the evil regime. "God's fate as a human responsibility" (p. 55).

Raphael draws upon the tradition of the Shekhinah to identify the imminence of God in the human encounter. "Shekhinah does not hide her face.... The Shekhinah indicates the real presence of a suffering God" (p. 54). To be specific in the care that love generates, in acts of beholding and embracing, God's face is restored. It is a human responsibility to bring God into Auschwitz in the manner one cares for another. The restoration of the human image of another creates the space for God to be present in relationality. Whether it is in the sharing of a few drops of water or using them to clean a face, or the handing off of a piece of life-saving bread, the restoration of humanity and the re-emergence of God are concurrently enacted. Specifically, "care revealed the likeness of God's personality that Auschwitz corroded and erased" (p. 60). The face of the Divine in the setting of demonic ordering "is a restoration of the obscured face of God" (p. 60). God is realized anew in the care of loving hands and human generosity is enacted. Humans can make room for God in settings she has been driven out of. Acts of caring can restore the face of God in the face of another. Even touching another could bring about restoration; create a space for the Divine presence. In a sense, Raphael contends one has the Holy in one's hands! By contrast, men tended to be cerebral. Interestingly, Raphael argues that, "Ordinary acts like the attempted washing or wiping of a face were, here, in the radical disruption of normal categories of actions and agenda, transposed into a sacred dimension in ways that might not have been (or be) the case outside of Auschwitz" (p. 80).

In acts of care the immanence of the transcended God is established. While the Nazi regime and regimen were calculated to drive God from the death camps, relationality brought Her back and enabled Her to suffer with the suffering. The form of God's power is to be present in the demonic without ceasing to be God. The self-giving of mortals creates the space in which God can once and again be present, and in the most de-humanizing settings. In the face of the other, God's image is restored. And the agenda of atomization is met with the connecting of mutual assistance and affirmation. Going out to meet the other is to be met by the Ultimate Other. And a form of liberation is encountered.

And that calls for a re-imaging of God. So, what does the face of God resemble? If one is to see God restored in the relational act, what image flashes forward? For some over time, perhaps most, it is a straight, white, male! Raphael delivers us from that and stipulates the consequences. She designates "him Father-God. The monarchical man of wars – was of little or no comfort" (p. 116). The omnipotent one is marked by failure. By contrast to the Father-God, "as Mother-God this God is ethically inter-pretive, interceptive, protective, and consoling" (p. 127). And the face of God is a suffering face in the midst of suffering. Maternal love is relentlessly present, willingly invested in the suffering. While the Father-God evidenced futility, the Mother-God could prevail against "the sterile cruelty inherent in the system" (p. 90). She is deathless in the face of death. Her maternal capacity and disposition to "keep together" fashioned a communal love of mutual care. "Looking away" is not an option for the Mother-God, neither does she resort to the abstractions, characterized by the male face of God. When women reached out to the other, reestablished relationality, the face of God was evident and resembled a maternal one. As the bearer of familial love and care she restored the one who was exiled by the death camp perspective. And the face of God is reconfigured.

The myth of God the Father survives in peaceful settings but not in the Holocaust. Is there a departure from the biblical tradition? God the Father echoes robustly but not exclusively – common practices and liturgies notwithstanding. The womb is a habitat where the human and Divine are joined. And upon a time the maternal God "Like a mother, has carried Israel" (Isaiah 46:3-4). God is a giver of the life according to the creation narrative. God gives birth to the world and all that is in it. Being there for the other is the matrix in which the Mother God reappears. There the face of God mirrors the mother who gives birth, cannot restrain compassion, and reaches out for reunion. What happened in Auschwitz was "the restoration (tikkun) of her divine image in women. Revelation in Auschwitz… was the reappearance of what disappeared," (p. 133) when persons in Auschwitz were face to face. The maternal face of God emerged and there was a Presence well beyond a "commanding voice." Where dignity is restored the face of God erased by the Nazis emerges and the wounds of God as well are healed (p. 149). The depths of Shekhinah are evident in the realization "there is no place she is not" (p. 154).

III

A caring presence trumps a commanding voice, does it not? "Never again" has merit but is it sufficient? While one would definitely not want to choose between hearing and seeing the Divine, would not seeing the Divine be preferable to hearing if one had to choose? And given the option, does the face have to be maternal?

Some might wonder if Melissa Raphael is Mary Daly in reverse: "If God is female, is female God" and a matriarchy replaces a patriarchy? Considering the centuries over which Eve was presumed to be created out of a spare part (rib of Adam) that would be a tempting reversal. By some broken calculus turnabout is fair play. Sallie McFague sets the equation judiciously with the blind reminder, "God is she and he and neither" (*Models of God*, p. 99). And her settling on God as "parent" (pp. 99 & 100) appears to be eminently judicious. Is Raphael culpable when she affirms the Mother God as opposed to Father God? In fairness, consider her text: it boldly affirms the qualities evident in the maternal but does not limit access to that image of the Divine.

As an aside, it is worth considering the scholarship of Phyllis Trible (*God and the Rhetoric of Sexuality*, p. 18). She argues that the Hebrew word for Adam really means "earth creature" and is free of gender stipulation. And then she calls forward the text where the gender differentiation occurs simultaneously: "male and female created he them." (Genesis 1:27) It is not a reach to speculate that Raphael would be at ease with both the claims of Trible and McFague. While Raphael focuses upon the experience of women in the Holocaust and surfaces their destructive behavior, she does not confine access to God to female experience. At a number of points she affirms that men were not inevitably monarchical. Women did not have exclusive juris-diction over articulating and relating to the "Mother God." The relational acts of women did not preclude implementation in men. While masculine sanctification of the Holocaust world... was far more cerebral" (*The Female Face of God in Auschwitz*, p. 22) and ordinary acts less loaded with sacred space, "...both men and women care in the image of a loving God whose covenant with us institutes relational commitment" (p. 87). The maternal is a more vivid and necessary conveyer. Hers is a theology of image and the maternal is inevitably more consequential in signifying the Divine in the midst of the demonic. Neither Raphael nor her God is exclusionary.

But that was then; is straight, white, male now the creation of a social reality that won't only prevail but is impervious to trans-formation? Perhaps the agenda should be to reclaim their mother and the maternal while subverting the domination of their father. Returning to the womb is not an option but immersing oneself in that image is a start in gender liberation. Our mother carried us for nine months while fathers were in and out somewhat briefly! Unfortunate memories may remain of not wanting to be a "mama's boy" (therefore sissy) which may be a risk but not an obstructive one. The life-giving care, and attendant discomfort, is not accessible to memory but could be to the imagination. In that imagination one could go home again and have a sample of what it takes to see the face of God in one's origination!

Straight, white, males, (and others) in Auschwitz could in the self-giving care of another restore the face of God; bring the reality of God into the death camps. Surely the Divine does not need the grossness of the demonic for us to see Her face; but the centrality of relationality is in our DNA and if we create space for the sacred She will be there. "In the maternal quality of divine love... is of a Mother-God known to tradition as (the) Shekhinah" (p. 117). Then a commanding voice will be at best a whisper, and the presence of a reality will prevail as human dignity is preserved and sustained in maternal-like caring.

To re-integrate femaleness and divinity "...is to restore God's power to God after its hubristic arrogation.... Those holocaustal moments when the human and the divine female face was cleansed of its patriarchal (dis) figuration... it is at the moment that the female human face can hold up a mirror to God that patriarchy has failed in its intention to cover God's face.... There were those who could lift the mirror and those who could not" (p. 160). There still are. And straight, white, males can be "born again" and then join "those who could lift the mirror" (p. 160) and see traces of the One who suffers and embraces our suffering. And demonic privilege is transformed into a liberating presence. That is the breakthrough of God.

Bibliography

Berenbaum, Michael. *After Tragedy and Triumph* (New York: Cambridge University Press, 1990).

Braiterman, Zachary. *(God) After Auschwitz* (New Jersey: Princeton University Press, 1998).

Fackenheim, Emil L. "The 614th Commandment," *Holocaust: Religion and Philosophical Implications*, eds. John K. Roth and Michael Berenbaum (Minnesota: Paragon House, 1989).

Fackenheim, Emil L. *God's Presence in History* (New York: Jason

Aronson Publishers, 1997).

Fackenheim, Emil L. *Quest for Past and Future* (Indiana: Indiana University Press, 1968).

Fackenheim, Emil L. "On Jewish Life After Auschwitz," in *Post-Holocaust Dialogues*, Stephen T. Katz (New York: New York University Press, 1985).

Fackenheim, Emil L. *The Jewish Bible after the Holocaust* (Indiana: Indiana University Press, 1990).

McFague, Sallie. *Models of God* (Philadelphia: Fortress Press, 1987).

Rapael, Mielissa. *The Female Face of God in Auschwitz* (London and New York: Routledge, 2003).

Trible, Phyllis. *God and the Rhetoric of Sexuality* (Philadelphia: Fortress Press, 1978).

Wyschogrod, Michael. "Faith and the Holocaust," *Judiasim*, 20, no.3 (summer 1971).

Chapter Six

When the Sacred Canopy Folds

Peter Berger wrote it in 1967 but the claim has staying power. While it is not uniquely related to the plight of straight, white males, the "crisis of theology" has not mellowed. In many settings, most explicitly the university, it has intensified and is more complex. Berger writes of it specifically in relation to religious institutions: "the problem...how to keep going in a milieu that no longer takes for granted their definition of reality" (*The Sacred Canopy*, p. 156). Initially he identified the villain as the prominence of pluralism which at least in part authorized secularization. One of Berger's most prominent articulations as a sociologist was to identify the nature of the social construction of reality and its expression in the legitimizing function of religion, the sense of a "sacred cosmos" authorizing some significant sense of permanence in the face of the construction of reality. Some things have an enhanced sense of reality as a consequence of religious legitimation. Yet that function is fading, at best "not taken for granted." To put it crudely the message of the church is contained in a leaky bucket! In our "milieu" it doesn't hold water! While Berger has retreated from his earlier assessment of secularization, the issue of "milieu" remains and the "definition of reality" has changed hands. Some say it has been passed over to the economy after a substantial sojourn in the sciences. If there is a "rising tide" for theology and institutional enterprises, it does not benefit the plight of the church, and in fact, it likely is not our tide! Given the "crisis in theology" how does the church embody and advocate in an era when other realities prevail?

I

If we draw attention to Moses again it is not because we think he is contemporary with the church! But he is a major player in the drama of the journey of a religious community. Moses is an exquisite model of emerging faithfulness in a setting that subverts it. He may not be a straight, white, male but the dilemma of privilege resides in his earlier years. John L. Markey in *Moses in Pharaoh's House* (p. 59) invites us to think about what he might have become rather than what he did. It well could have been a different story, with severe consequences for his people.

> What if Moses, instead of developing a strong sense of empathy and compassion for others, had grown up feeling both increasingly entitled and yet victimized by his "unfair" association with the lower-class socially outcast Hebrews? What if Moses enjoying the luxury of being a member of Pharaoh's house, began to feel that he wasn't receiving his share of status? What if Moses developed a deep resentment toward the Hebrew people and came to detest them as somehow depriving him of the fullness of respect and attainment of riches to which he felt entitled?

The journey of the Hebrew people would have been different; he might even have achieved status by ridding the kingdom of them. But privilege was not a defining detriment. How radically different the religious communities, then and now, likely would have been. One can in fact be in a world but not of it, and Moses is a prime witness of a Passover that might have become a pushover!

Perhaps we could get our bearings from another event centuries later but strangely similar. Reincarnation is not something biblically warranted but there is more than a little of Moses' DNA in the Christ event. But we need to see it on Easter morning. While some churches have historically privileged the male disciples, interestingly we are not told where they vanished to; clearly they "ducked out." It was two women, low of status in that era, who approached the empty tomb. You have to wonder what they expected; likely it was to do Jesus' body the respect it had been denied. It is not difficult to imagine his disciples thought he might have been taken to heaven! Now there was a "young man" at the tomb, not a disciple for sure. "More than one scholar has noticed that the instructions of the young man to the women at the tomb at the end of Mark are told: 'go back to Galilee where you will meet Jesus'" (Maia L. Kotrosits and Hal T. Taussig, *Re-reading the Gospel of Mark Amidst Loss and Trauma*, p. 161). That is when it all began and the line of T.S. Eliot comes to mind, "in the end is the beginning."

Galilee is not a random location! Some say it defines Jesus. To say it was a place of rebellion and resistance would only begin to tell the story of the return of Jesus there. In the parables Jesus had pitched God's Kingdom "in ordinary settings of Galilee, but always with socially subversive undertones" (Douglas Oakman, *The Political Aims of Jesus*, p. 73). Hence, Jesus going home there was treasonous and unpatriotic to say the least. Power every-where prevailed but resistance was remarkably evident as well. And it had a history. Richard A. Horsley notes that the reason Galilean-rebellion was so persistent "was the prominence of resistances to oppressive alien rule in Israelite tradition" (*Jesus and Empire*, p. 37). Indeed, prophets announcing that God was delivering them from foreign domination inspired them to fight...." Resistance to Herod had a trajectory; and it climaxed in Jesus. Galilee was in a sense the front line of control, and of rigorous resistance to it. Luke's gospel surfaces the charge of the Romans that Jesus was "perverting our nation... from Galilee to this place (Jerusalem)" (Luke 23:2). Jesus challenged the "economic deprivation and political subordination" that had marked the ethos in which Galileans functioned (Mark Lewis

Liberating Privilege

Taylor, *The Executed God*, p. 73). They were, he notes, "living sacrifices to a system where local elites... joined with the imperial system of Rome..." (p. 74). The daily struggle of Galilee to hold on to their land in the face of indebtedness defined the social reality of Galileans. Taxes took their toll as well; their collection was in the Temple by the state appointed Priests; and Jesus had the audacity to announce its impending destruction. To seek Jesus after crucifixion in the streets of Galilee was to name his ongoing reality as one of resistance to oppression. The journey of Jesus to Galilee was anything but safe. It is not ours to know who the young man was, but he certainly knew where Jesus was and where we are meant to be. And from Moses we are assured that it is possible to exist as a community "that got the hint." Being comfortable with prevailing injustice is not an option; and with a commitment to live in the reality of the Gospel, "they cannot accept the world as it is" (James Cone, *A Black Theology of Liberation*, p. 130).

II

Any disposition to be discontent is surfaced by an alternative reality. What Jesus proclaimed and embodied in Galilee was the reign of God and the promise it would prevail. In Berger's language, an unwillingness to internalize triggers the need for a new externalization. In the teachings and in the parables the Coming of the Kingdom spelled the demise of the prevailing order. A new social construction was at hand, and authenticated this time by the God of the Exodus and the Resurrection. Humans in community engaged in a "world-building enterprise" (*The Sacred Canopy*, p. 19) but the legitimizing of it is from beyond. As Berger continues: "Religion legitimates so effectively because it relates the precarious reality construction of empirical societies with ultimate reality" (p. 31). It was the gift of Jesus to embody and provoke an alternative reality, the contours of which

110

mimicked the mission of Jesus. The creation of a counter order "depends upon the presence of social structures within this reality… [which are] taken for granted and with which successive generations of individuals are socialized in such a way that their world will be real to them" (p. 46). And this brings us to the centrality of ritual.

While acknowledging the existence of "ritual boredom", Tom Driver maintains that "rituals have invented us" (*The Magic of Rituals*, p. 30). They are agents of transition and bold reminders; and they are agents of social change. Something is made present in rituals, engages us in imagining new futures and integrates us into their reality. They introduce us to an alternative territory which can become sacred and serve as a "focusing lens" (p. 48). We see differently if we have really engaged in the ritual. It is finally an engaging performance which nourishes alternative visions. In a real sense, something is produced and calls for implementation, embodiment. And ritual is integral to the divine – human encounters in history. Without them we are non-persons immersed in a non-history. To live in ritual is to come alive in liberation.

This brings the argument directly to the practice of the Eucharist. In much contemporary practice it is a socially harmless exercise largely encapsulated in individualistic agendas. It is the premier agent of spirituality. Pious feelings protrude and give ultimate assurances. One might even feel at peace having ingested the bread and the wine. Some of those privileged agendas might be legitimate but have to be countered by the event in context. In "the New Testament… meal gatherings are loaded with proclamation and contestation of social dynamics… rituals per se may indeed have a great deal to do with social order and change" (Taussig, *In the Beginning Was the Meal*, p. 20). The original event clearly was informed by the Passover but struggled and was propelled beyond it. There was to be sure "the last supper" and Rome would have its way the next day. But the celebration of the Passover as a setting gave it a political dimension. The Egyptians were defeated by One who was ahead of the Israelites "in the clouds" and pressed on to a promised land. The Egyptians did drown in the Red Sea and the cross itself was neutered as an exercise in terrorizing by an empty tomb. That was hardly good news in the Royal courts.

The authentic celebration of the Eucharist is anything but otherworldly, except when it has been domesticated by the interests of a prevailing order. There it has been raped and becomes an agent of the *status quo*. Recipients are passive, the elements harmless, and the Jesus event elsewhere! Only political desperation and divisiveness could separate the ritual settings from the struggle of the Israelites for liberation. Then it has become a sacralization as the love of Christ has been severed from his ministry to the marginals and his challenges of the prevailing order. The Eucharist should call to memory "he gave his life for the liberation of others. He was killed because he championed justice, truth, the poor, and the exploited" (Tissa Balasuriya, *The Eucharist and Human Liberation*, p. 80). And he goes on to proclaim "the Eucharist has to be related positively to human liberation if it is to be faithful to its origins and its performances" (p. 12). It is saluting the flag in reverse!

To taste the bread and wine, remembering what they represent, is to embrace an agenda counter to that of the prevailing order. If the Eucharist were perceived as unpatriotic its celebration would be more authentic. "...the very act of raising the cup to Jesus had elements of resistance" (Hal Taussig p. 120). The flag by the altar is a real sacralization. Singing "Onward Christian soldiers marching as to war, with the cross of Jesus marching on before" is evidence patriotism has obscured piety. The taking of the bread and wine, ingesting the sacrifice of Christ, should create political dissidents and shake the foundations of the prevailing order. For the act of Christ folds a sacred canopy inflated by the State and proclaims one marked by a suffering servant and a suffering God. What is being affirmed is commitment to an order of love and justice which dismantles one of profit and privilege. The Eucharist in context emboldens the weak and dismantles the powerful. It replaces the privatized version of "stand your ground" with "stand for the liberation of your neighbor". To be true to Jesus, one would have to take the bread and wine with fear and trembling. If one is not committed to changing the world, they should have the integrity to remain in a pew and salute the flag instead.

Straight, white, males may not be ready for that! But if they get a taste of Jesus at the altar they will never be the same – and neither will be the world and its privileges they have forsaken. A revitalized Eucharist could re-inflate a sacred canopy fashioned by Jesus. And transform a platitudinous claim for personal peace into an act at its origin one of civil disobedience.

III

If we move from the altar back to its origin in Scripture we are on the cusp of the generation of what Walter Brueggemann calls a "counter-imagination" (*Truth Speaks to Power*, p. 89), a form of discourse and persuasion which is subversive of the prevailing, totalizing, and absolutizing ruling order. But what is unique, perhaps, about this agenda is that it exploits the language and artifacts of the imperial order, some say the empire. The conventional wisdom is that the emperor's tools are not weapons of choice for disarming the emperor's regime. That bit of wisdom was not in circulation when the biblical writers were creating their narrative! Their task of redirecting privilege and emasculating power was transacted with an agenda of blatant theft! Their tactic was to exploit the master's book for the purposes of creating the "counter-imagination". It is safe to say they borrowed recklessly if not deviously from the imperial realities and rhetoric around them. The result was an erosion of power and a diminishment of privilege. And communication was indisputable because of its familiarity.

That is not so unusual when one considers how "intertwined" their existence was "with the Empire's visual world and the imagery created by and for its ruler" (Harry O. Maier, *Picturing Paul in Empire*, p. 4). With an agenda of persuasion, it is not so remarkable that one would invoke and imitate the vocabulary and imagery at hand (p. 6). If one is submerged in available discourse and imagery, it is not so unproductive that it would be employed –and eventually subvert it. A linguistic theft is virtually unavoidable. But what is evident with biblical writers is that the emperor's tools were used to subvert the emperor's order. A liberating imagination can provoke viewers into an action dramatically opposed to Caesar's realm. In the process "re-imagination" occurs. The language and imagery is adopted for agendas, alien to the original intent. The outcome is a rather "imperial hybridity" (p. 33). That which is alien to the Gospel becomes a vehicle of its expression. Writing about Paul in particular, Harry O. Maier claims that "the power of his persuasion lies in its ability to draw on the world of imperial imagery and civic vocabulary, only to revise it so that the visual world that such imagery usually describes now becomes a vehicle for imagery a wholly different world" (p. 51). That is, the Gospel is encoded in discourse at odds with its purposes! To invoke again the language of John C. Scott, a "public transcript" of domination becomes an instrument for expressing the subversion of it by a "hidden transcript" (p. 36). And the consequence is the demise of what presumed to be a "sacred" canopy.

A theologian, Mark Lewis Taylor, in *"The Executed God*, (pp. 82-83) makes vivid use of this. Taylor claims that "Paul takes some of the dearest terms of his discourse from the imperial world, then bends them back upon the claims of empire to champion the greater power of the way of Jesus" (p. 82). The Greek word for "gospel" has its origin in celebration of military accomplishments. Jesus' bringing of "salvation" in the empire refers to earthly politics in which the imperial order prevails. The Greek word for "faith" in the public realm is linked to loyalty to the realm. Again, the Greek word for "Lord" in the Roman discourse would suggest domination by the Caesars of the world. And imagery for the coming again of Jesus is borrowed from that of a King or Emperor. Even the references to peace are borrowed from the State and its determination to insure "law and order." Ironically, Jesus and his message are understood in discourse appropriate for the Empire but now distinguish and contradict it. The words do not have the same meaning when severed from their origin to reveal what contradicts them. The most egregious theft is the cross of Jesus, his crucifixion by the State. That State has no power greater than what is symbolized by the cross. In biblical times it was situated at popular intersections so that "the people" would note that ultimate power over life and death resided in the civic order. But, the church, as noted before, had the audacity to place it on the altar and designate it as the ultimate evidence that God prevails in history. That this is a "suffering God" on the cross determined to work God's purposes in the public sphere is a final claim upon who really prevails and where some who choose to genuflect at appropriate points in public service do so, it is an act of defiance of the public order. Genuflection is every bit as political as the Eucharist. In fact, they are siblings of a Parent in heaven. It is not hard to imagine persons recoiling from the act when its political dimension is in evidence. Rather than "rally around the flag" it becomes "submit to the elements." Liberation is not in patriotism but in the break-through of God enacted at the table with liberative elements.

This argument could be seen as a diversion from the issue of straight, white, males. But the biblical record rightly understood has a way of invading the realms of power and privilege and dissolving their claim. This is to contend that those of us with "the world on our side" can be the target of the biblical narrative.

This is to contend that being on the wrong side of God's history can creep into consciousness. The Gospel is tramping on our territory with the very vocabulary and images with which we have secured a safe place. The biblical writers used the language of the day to announce the demise of its intended realm. What was intended to signify the end of the Jesus event in fact signaled its climax. Death was put to death! The emperor's tools achieved the emperor's demise. In Paul's discourse it had the advantage of being "immediately recognizable" (Maier, p. 151).

This is to affirm for straight, white, males that their realm and "sacred" canopy has been dismantled and a new "counter-imagination" is at large and in play; the presumptive power and privilege have been dead and buried with no hope of a resurrection on the third day. Look in the mirror for evidence it is over. This is to claim that the recognition the emperor has no claims is to stumble upon one's own nakedness! And in terms images thought to have cosmic certitude. This is to contend that the possible liberation of the benefactors of an order constructed to their benefit alone virtually self-destructed with language thought to be assuring their invulnerability. When the veil is lifted and the masks disintegrate, solidity with those have been designated "other" has the character of a new identity committed to a new order. "Counter-imagination" calls for a world in which human flourishing is enabled and one can feel at home in one's own reality in a community of mutual authentication. You can embrace who you are when confronted by whom you are not.

This is to reveal that the privileged are vulnerable. Their confidence has been eroded by reversals that are transformative. Privilege becomes a burden one can do without! When a "counter-imagination" is at work, the defenses which have secured privilege and power become permeable and even in time welcoming. So the injunction to become who Jesus intends you to be begins to form and the shackles of privilege begin to fold leaving one porous. Then being a straight, white, male can become a place to be faithful and embody the realities the cross and resurrection fulfill. The very coherence and purpose evident in the Eucharist takes form in territory thought immune to it. One can leave the table empowered to become a straight, white, male in the image of Christ! The power and privilege become servants of a new world. Authentic selfhood under the jurisdiction of Jesus evokes the designation of straight, white, males to be honorific and authentic rather than desecrating and diminishing. Then this divestiture of privilege and power enables one to be "in it" without being "of it". One can indeed divert it without leaving it. One can even re-construct a new sacred canopy on the ashes of a former one!

The issue front and center is of self-identity and the presumption a straight, white, male has no possibility of "getting it right". To the degree he is suffocating in privilege and power, the goals of a liberation theology will be preempted. Acts of solidarity are the pathway to a biblically centered theology. But Scripture has another option. And it is created by the very factors that disqualify the straight, white, male. As has been argued, Moses escaped the denunciation and contamination of his setting. Miriam has a discerning moment, or series of them, of clarity and conviction. And the centurion at least had a moment of lucidity. It has been argued that the biblical writers, Paul in particular, were enabled to "get it right" as the language of privilege and power became a servant of authentic disclosure. And in that intersection of imperial rhetoric the light can shine that illumines who Jesus really is and what his mission is unambiguously about. The irony is that what conceals also reveals! One's fouled location can become an asset of sorts. If the transferal of the language of privilege and power is secured to understand the Gospel, its demise is disclosed and its "sacred" canopy folds. Even as it illumines who Jesus is, it is as divested as a reality before the Holy One. And we may be free to see both who we are and what we can become in the presence of God's purposes. One has the option of seeking shelter under another sacred canopy, one inflated by the Jesus reality.

Harry O. Maier calls attention to the last words of Paul in his letter to the Colossians, "Remember my chains" (4:18) represents "a vivid picture that speaks a thousand words" (p. 63). It was after all a letter from jail and was invoking a "social memory" by when the apostle called attention to struggle and opposition Paul endured. And it was for Maier an invitation to include "a second generation of Christ's followers to frame their lives by way of a social memory" (p. 64). And it may well have been understood as an imitation of Christ's suffering. But is it not possible that Paul had in mind as well another figurative "claim". The early years of Paul were ones when he was on the wrong side of the Jesus events. Then there was the episode on the Damascus road where Saul was called to account for persecuting Jesus. And that is a "social memory" as well as an invitation for a dramatic reversal in Saul's/Paul's relationship to the Jesus events. Then that is a "social memory" which invites straight, white, males to divest their claims and embrace a "counter-imagination". What was understood about Jesus evoked the vocabulary of the prevailing order? Maier reminds us that "as Colossians, Ephesians uses imperial language and metaphors to describe the benefits of Christ's reign, the imperial situation Ephesians creates and imagines a church as the place where the social goals of concord and moral transformation are achieved" (p. 103). Perhaps this identifies the church as the place where "double consciousness" persists and the transaction between being straight, while, males and who we are in Christ is negotiated. And while each has staying power, the cross and resurrection determine who will triumph. Ironically, again, it is the language of the imperial order that disputes it. "Colossians describes the death of Christ as a triumph over "principalities and power" (p. 69). There is only one sacred canopy that never folds. There liberation is in the form of the breakthrough of God.

Bibliography

Balasuriya, Tissa. *The Eucharist and Human Liberation*. (Maryknoll, NY: Orbis Books, 1979).

Berger, Peter L. *The Sacred Canopy*. (Garden City, NY: Doubleday, 1967).

Brueggemann, Walter. *Truth Speaks to Power*. (Louisville, KY: Westminster John Knox Press, 2013).

Cone, James H. *A Black Theology of Liberation*. (Mary Knoll: Orbis Books, 1986).

Driver, Tom F. *The Magic of Ritual*. (New York: Harper Collins, 1991).

Horsley, Richard A. *Jesus and Empire*. (Minneapolis, MN: Fortress Press, 2003).

Kotrosits, Maia, and Hal Taussig. *Re-reading the Gospel of Mark Amidst Loss and Trauma*. (New York: Palgrave MacMillan 2013).

Maier, Harry O. *Picturing Paul in Empire*. (New York: Bloomsbury 2013).

Markey, John J. *Moses in Pharaoh's House*. (Winona MINN Anselm Academic 2013).

Moltmann, Jürgen. *Theology of Hope*. (New York: Harper & Row, 1967).

Oakman, Douglas E. *The Political Aims of Jesus*. (Minneapolis: Fortress Press, 2012).

Taussig, Hal. *In the Beginning Was the Meal*. (Minneapolis (Minn.): Fortress Press, 2009).

Taylor, Mark L. *The Executed God*. (Minneapolis. MN.: Fortress Press, 2001).

Warnock, Raphael G. *The Divided Mind of the Black Church*. (New York: NYU Press, 2013).

Chapter Seven

The Church as Subversive Community

Many theologians, some would say the most authentic of them, center their theological journey in the church. From Karl Barth to James Cone, it is the setting in which God is invested and its agenda for the world is subversive. The faith and the community of faith are inseparable, though contention is more common than collusion. In the timeline between Barth and Cone, Robert McAfee Brown frequently challenged aspiring ministers with this mission: "It is time for the church to strip down for action." The task of clergy was to enable the church to divest baggage that impairs its mission and distorts its message. In the 1950s the church was flourishing: sanctuaries were overflowing (and expanding!), sermons preached in prestigious New York City churches were summarized in the *New York Times,* and the biblical tradition was often translated into "feel good" agendas. No wonder Martin Luther King, while deeply immersed in the faith, would charge that the American church had a "weak, ineffectual voice with an uncertain sound" (quoted in Benjamin T. Lynerd, *Republican Theology,* p. 181). The Gospel had been muted, some would say raped. Stripping down for action, advocated by theologian Brown, alone could purge the baggage society had blended with the message.

Walter Brueggemann was in the classroom of Dr. Brown and one could speculate he got the message. Decades later Brueggemann would refer to the process as "enculturation." The tradition has been compromised. "There is a depreciation of memory and a ridicule of hope" (*The Prophetic Imagination,* p. 1). "The offense of the Gospel" was purged and scarcely an echo remained. As an institution the church had become a comfortable presence, its message pleasant and palatable. Very few stark and disturbing words protrude. Peace with the world had become negotiated – on the world's terms. In some measure going to church was indistinguishable from going to Rotary or even the country club. The overlap in constituency, agenda, and message was significant, even revealing. While the religiously successful would proclaim that religion had gotten modern, the students who heard Dr. Brown claim it had merged with modernity.

It may not be too bold to suggest it was initially crafted and implemented by straight, white, males. They were in the pulpits, in the pews, and on the boards engineering a revival, which bore slight resemblance to anything Jesus would have identified with! Given that allegation, how might one now claim that straight, white, males could be central in "stripping down for action" and perhaps birthing the re-emergence of authentic faith? On the other hand, why not? Biblical precedence has been articulated in previous chapters.

I

One might embrace that task by initiating a distinction, perhaps an unlikely one: there is a difference between standing up *for* the faith and standing up *to* the faith (as represented). The first is more common, often heroic; the second is uncommon and often perceived as rude! Yet one is not to be preferred to the other. Standing up to the faith may seem more problematic. "Can't we all just get along?" has dimensions of a sacred hymn. Being nice can become an imperative and all the more so in the religious arena.

Standing up to the faith has biblical warrant, uncomfortable even stark over time. But it is agenda setting for the church. Consider the Syrophoenician woman and her tasteless rebuke of Jesus. Sharon Ringe claims that she "trips him up and corrects him" (quoted from *Faith and Feminism*, Diane B. Lipsett and Phyllis Trible, ed., p. 73). The woman had the audacity to stand up to Jesus' response, blatantly call him out. She is not a straight, white, male but she could be a role model for the church. While hardly a perfect fit, her act was swiftly embraced by Jesus and therefore authoritative.

Here is the story. It is rather brief: Mark 7:25-30. Her cause and her love were understandable. The Mother's child was a victim of an evil spirit and she pleaded that Jesus would cast it out. Nothing unreasonable about that. What Mother wouldn't invoke whatever powers she perceived as available? But the response was: "let the children first be fed, for it is not right to take the children's bread and throw it under the table" (vs. 27). There would seem to be a compassion deficit in that, and the Mother names it graciously. "Yes, Lord; yet even the dogs under the table eat the children's crumbs" (vs. 28). That did it! She was clever enough to acknowledge his claim while challenging its consequences! Jesus sent her home where she found her child liberated from the demon. Clearly the woman stood up to Jesus and he reordered his priorities. For saying that, Jesus got back on message. Did she not cause Jesus to "strip down for action?"

It was less than gracious of Jesus to suggest the Syrophoenician woman was a "dog." To his credit, he backed off when she reacts with the tart response that even the dogs have the children's crumbs under the table. He pivots on that. But why does her rejoinder seem so harsh? She is gracious in the contention that images do not apply to her and her daughter, but firm in her appeal. One can respond in two directions. Clues emerge which suggest she was of an exploitative class, elite, and indifferent to the very kind of needs she was addressing. Symbolically Jesus is calling for attention to the social needs her and "her kind" have ignored. Her privileges have translated into exploitative agendas with peasants in Galilee. In an abrupt manner, Jesus was saying, "I know your kind." And you are asking for the very attention to needs you have denied. But the reaction of Jesus cuts in another direction as well. His impatience yields to dialogue and transformation. Jesus yields to a Mother's plea. Dialogue has occurred. They connected. And her claim is honored.

It is too easy to dismiss the Syrophoenician woman as uppity. She called out Jesus and enabled a healing transaction to occur. And she is, as suggested, a model for what the church needs. She can be seen as evidence that perhaps even straight, white, males can set the record straight, strip down for action, and enable the faith community to right its course. Granted, she was desperate; her child was at risk. But is it beyond imagination to conceive of straight, white, males having a moment of self-awareness bordering on desperation? The challenge of theologian Brown to aspiring clergy in reality fell on the ears of straight, white, males – Brueggemann and this author as well. While Brueggemann labels the uncultured as "numb" that does not necessarily mean deaf! With the intervention of the Holy Spirit an authentic Word can land on territory less than welcoming.

It would be a reach to suggest Jesus was a straight, white, male! Clearly male, but likely of color. However, the Syrophoenician woman called him out and got him back on message. And with inordinate speed. Why would it be unthinkable that straight, white, males would be instrumental in stripping down the church for action? Nothing ultimately stands in the way of joining Walter Brueggemann in standing up to the faith as practiced in the society. Divesting enculturation is a possibility, perhaps riding more on the Holy Spirit than the human one!

This is to suggest that "stripping down" means rescuing the faith from what the seepage of societal values has accomplished. One could start at the beginning with the birth of Jesus as embraced by the church. The event reeks of sentimentality and with harmless dimensions. The "little Lord Jesus" of the hymns is adorable (and always white). The shepherds are onlookers, verifying the appropriateness of the event. Never mind that they were "social junk" in their time. The manger is sanitized, at best inconvenient. And the angels made a charming choir. The animals cooperate and are uncommonly passive. Typically, Mary is white, blond, and unambiguously wholesome. When God comes to earth She is cuddly. So the hymn reminds us that "the hopes and fears of all the years are met in thee tonight." Really?

What would the event be like if it was reclaimed on its own terms, in its own time and circumstances? What would stripping down for action look like? Christmas at "St. Whatever" bears little resemblance to the original event. Start with the fact that the times were more severe than now when Congress and the President are at odds. Caesar Augustus, Quirinius, Tiberius, Pilate, and Herod are not duly elected officials in a democratic society! They are "imperial officials who *think* they are in charge of history" and will do anything to execute their rule (Chad M. Myers & Matthew C. Colwell, *Our God is Undocumented*, p. 174). And the Holy Family was driven from their homeland by a census which was an agent of taxation. Clearly it is a "displacement" (p. 175) which serves the economic agenda of the establishment. The adoration of the shepherds is charming but one needs to remember they are the "lowest of the low" in the time of the event. One can imagine the equivalent now but naming them might be precarious! Giving birth in the garage of the time is less than honorific. The Holy Family is incongruously displaced. The angelic choir adds charm but what they are singing is highly political, even subversive. "Glory to God in the highest and on earth peace" is spiritually uplifting until we realize it was "applied exclusively to Caesar Augustus" (p. 175) and therefore was a defiant claim of "another King." Then there is the recognition that Mary was an unwed Mother and his Father fades out in time. In short, the privileges are conspicuously absent and the ruling order threatened by a choir. And we need to remember that Herod "got it" and feigned interest in coming to worship Jesus but later assassinated all male babies to liquidate possible competition.

The rescue of the original event of Christmas would situate the investment of God in unlikely places with purposes at odds with the ruling order. Straight, white, males have an authentic opportunity to stand up to the distorting of the faith and strip down for action. The message of the church needs to be re-configured! To subvert the enculturation would enable the Word to be heard. Liberating Christmas is a worthy place to begin. Standing up to the faith would make clear the location of God in the world and where the church is called to be. And whom it is called to be among. In most locations that would not be "good news."

II

Clearly, this is to suggest the church is called to be a counter community, oppositional in its message, and even subversive in its actions. It may be particularly appropriate and ironic, that straight, white, males could be instrumental in that mission. Privilege need not be encapsulating, as has been argued. One can divest, strip down, and function from realities that do not currently exist. Corinthians holds up "faith, hope, and love." The first and the last get a fair run in the implementation of the tradition. But hope? Unless it is falsely channeled into optimism, it is the fainter voice. Real hope is grounded in something beyond the moment with priority given to what is arriving.

The church is a counter community where the future is its sense of reality, where the social reality is not what is at hand, and that there is "a *new day* beyond this unbearable day" (Walter Brueggemann, *Ice Axes For Frozen Seas*, p. 108). At its authentic best, the church exists in stories at odds with the prevailing narrative. And that is "intrinsically subversive" (p. 113). More commonly it yields to "Egyptianization" (p. 144) and engages in alliances with the present. If you leave and have not been offended, there could be a Gospel deficit. The Theology of Hope did not emerge from Wall Street, the Country Club, or the White House. Jürgen Moltmann found the priority of hope in the hopelessness of a prison camp as he was exposed to texts he had previously ignored.

Scripture has an obsession with cries of desperation, voices that name what is at hand as intolerable. And some struggle and are perplexed by the faithlessness. Whether it is the Israelites "crying out" to God about their oppression or Jesus on the cross naming abandonment, the presumption is that all there is is hopelessness and despair. And the Psalmist gives voice to its existence: "By the waters of Babylon, there we sat down and there we wept..." (Psalm 137). And then the question, "How can we sing the Lord's song in a foreign land?" (Psalm 137:4). But there is something to be retrieved in each scenario. Consider what is stealthily concealed. It is in nightmares that the theme emerges, "I have a Dream." These are the cries of desperation, the recognition of "a future beyond these intractable facts," one grounded in "divine resolve" (p. 108) defines the reality in which one is called to live. At best the church is the community that affirms an "arriving future" in which ultimacy is upended. The role of the prophet is to call into play "the future as gift" (p. 108). The journey to a Promised Land is evidence of it as well as an empty tomb.

Privilege is seductive and straight, white, males are typically susceptible and therefore submerged in it. But not inevitably so. They can provoke the church to become addicted to the future, and "abound in hope." And this means a willingness to declare the present outrageous. The counter community in its obsession with the future is giving voice to the violence in the present arrangements. Hope is inherently subversive. That is why Herod acted to liquidate "another King." And why the religious community put Jesus on the cross. Privilege may have a demonic dimension but it need not be deaf to what is intolerable. If the church strips down for action, it will be a threat to the prevailing order. When the church is "the place to go" for peace and goodwill it has violated the faith. As a counter community it lifts up what is deemed acceptable in the prevailing order and exposes it through an "arriving future."

The church is called to be a community of inclusion. And straight, white, males are called to be agents of it. Victimizers can divest. Hope contradicts; the faithful put their lives on the line, at least their reputations! The future that arrives from God does not tolerate a world in which children die of hunger, in which those who labor faithfully cannot afford necessities, in which violence is the answer to apparently intractable circumstances, in which those who are sexually different are discriminated against, in which the homeless are "frozen stiff" on park benches, in which accumulation drives fiscal discrimination, in which health care is designed for those who can afford it, and in which justice is at the mercy of those with the means to pay for it. The future arriving from the God of Jesus calls into existence a counter community of inclusion and a determination to implement it.

In the 14th Chapter of Luke Jesus has been invited to "the house of a ruler" (vs. 1), the establishment and supporters of the prevailing order. And among other transactions, he lectured them on the formation of a quest list, what one might look like if defined by the future. In the parable he admonished him not to invite his friends, relatives, or business associates. The summons is to "...listen to voices too weak to be heard on political platforms, in parliament, boardrooms, or military tribunals" (Mercy Amba Oduyoye, *Daughters of Anowa*, p. 206). He said, "When you give a feast, invite the poor, the maimed, the lame, the blind, and you will be blessed..." (vs.13). When the future defines reality propriety is subverted and a new agenda is in play. How would one establish the case that straight, white, males cannot be penetrated (some would say perverted!) by the message of Jesus? Stripping down for action changes the constituency, the agenda, and the outcome.

The elevation of hope is transformative. Mercy Amba Oduyoye from within her setting in Africa, writes about being "at home with the future" (Obuyoye, p. 206-207). And harkening to the Book of Revelation she writes, "The new is already here, we do not have to go up to heaven, heaven has come down to meet us. If only we have eyes to see, we can observe God walking among us" (p. 206-207). That is an arriving future which can be lived into reality. And by the grace of God, it is not beyond the reach of straight, white, males. They (we) have only to embrace the gift, boldly proclaim, and live it.

III

While Cornel West argued that Martin Luther King has been "santaclausified," the image could have been directed as well at representations of God. She now became "a jolly old man with a smile giving out toys to everyone from right-wing Republicans, to centrists, to progressives" (*Black Prophetic Fire*, p. 76). The God of the Exodus and the Resurrection has been refashioned. In the interests of a few, the reality of the many is now silenced by a God whose characteristic is "do no harm." Straight, white, males have had a role in that silencing and now can embrace the agenda of "stripping down" until the biblical God surfaces. That God "comes down to meet us" (p. 206) more often than not in unsavory places with subversive agendas.

On more than one occasion Walter Brueggemann has quoted from a letter to a friend crafted by Kafka: "...I think we ought to read only books that bite and sting us...[that] shake us awake like a blow to the skull... a book must be the ax for the frozen sea within us" (*Ice Axes For Frozen Seas*, p. 1). Substitute the word God for book and Brueggemann's historic agenda is evident. He might want to clarify that "within" applies to persons and the social realities within which they function. God's melting is without bounds or duration.

One of the things that distinguish the biblical God from false gods is that She can be fully present in the extremities of existence without diminishing what makes Her God. As Raphael writes, "she could consent to be defiled by virtue of her immanence and still be God..." (p. 85). Unlike Joseph, God is not tempted by "Egyptianization," though Her followers often are! One cannot melt the "frozen sea" with systems and individuals who exempt God from immersion in the settings that freeze and immobilize. God is even at home in our "matrices of deep despair" (Brueggemann, p. 47) whether the context is a prison camp or college dormitory. The agency of God seeks out the crucibles of human existence and implants hope. The biblical God is not primarily present for cuddling but for transforming the need for it.

The God of the Exodus and the Resurrection is one who not only melts the frozen within but transforms the world that creates it. She is present as the author of a "counter possibility" (p. 6). She creates the possibility of over stepping what entraps and cripples. The one who "made fools of the Egyptians," (p. 369) confronts the world of enslavement and crucifixion. Fear is then sucked out of the lives of the marginalized and planted squarely in the centers of power. Ultimately the Pharaohs and Herods have a meltdown. And what empowers resistance and revolution is the relationship Raphael identified.

The characteristic of life experiences for straight, white, males is that their (our) social reality is settled. The values, institutions, and ethics are fashioned to their interests. Agitation is uncommon; living in an "eternal now" creates life experiences which are predictable, safe, and comfortable. Amnesia in relation to the future prevails. But the faith community, in the measure it lives authentically, is one drawn by issues of departure from the prevailing order. Stripping down for action is threatening and not a priority! The "frozen sea within" is not in the market for turmoil. The impulse to "turn up the heat" is silenced by the reigning social realities. The "counter possibility" does not self-create. But the people of the Exodus and the Resurrection have a memory. In the measure it is not tarnished and diminished; at the center of it is a God who is merciless in relation to the "frozen seas." She listens to the weak voices, She embraces the pain which impairs them, and She acts boldly and perhaps recklessly. To the prevailing order that God is outrageous and the search for false gods prevails. The biblical God has no patience with settled social relations and at Her best disturbs and unsettles them. One can imagine the mood of Pharaoh as the Israelites were led out of captivity by Moses and One "ahead of them in the clouds." And certainly the King was confident Jesus was "handled" on the cross but an empty tomb established otherwise. One can control the way God is imagined but not the God beyond imagination! While Rome has no tolerance for opposition, neither does the biblical God.

Straight, white, males in a subversive community can become comfortable with a disruptive God! While some might say, "that is unlikely," with a nudge from the Holy Spirit and gaze fixed on the God who has the future as Her essential reality, opposition can be permanent. It can be the new eternal now. Straight, white, males can resist the "frozen seas" within us and the institutions we create, fashion a future in keeping with the Ultimate Agenda of God. The church can be driven by the faith that "the arc of God's governance is long" (Brueggemann, p. 255) and prevails. Nothing abates it. The biblical God is out of control. And departure from the prevailing order is an agenda the biblical God sets and we may yield to.

This raises the question of articulating what the world would be like with an outrageous God at the center. The prophets of old were bold in their proclamation but their constituency had a memory less prominent now. Not always, however, was the narrative of God boldly in play. Consider the Book of Hebrews.

As interpreted by Jason Whitlark in *Resisting Empire*, the author was artful in the narrative. The author of Hebrews spoke to "second generation Christians" (p. 9) in which some amnesia was at play. While it might be presumed to be a Gentile audience, the target community, the imperial order was pervasive, lowering the volume at best and shooting it down at worst. Whitlark argues that the author engaged in a "rhetorical form of figured or covert allusion" (p. 21). Its nature "intends something more than what he or she actually says" (p. 27). Saying it directly or too plainly was dangerous in relation to imperial powers and an audience protected by some denial or amnesia. Speaking openly was dangerous but also less than strategic to the intended audience. The agenda of the audience was to tease out what was intended. The issue now might not be the state but the prevailing order which had shut down oppositional moves and deafened the ears of the community.

There is no compelling reason to assume that straight, white, males advocating the church move toward a counter community are under imperial threats. But the resistance evident in the time of the Scripture is relevant and the reality of amnesia exists as well. Hence, figurative rhetoric is the game to play.

IV

In an earlier chapter we explored the interaction of religion and the economic order. Here we want to explore more pragmatically the ways in which the church might address the market economy in the light of the economy of God – and do so with "figuration" where intent trumps assertion. Stark and blatant attacks could be necessary but aren't the only form of enabling the contrast to protrude. Focusing on the texture of God could be more subtle and play out a figurative agenda. Then the consequences can be teased out by the audience without entering into adversarial discourse. One might think of it as similar to the familiar "bait and hook!"

A seemingly unlikely and apparently harmless theme with which to begin is an exploration of the Sabbath prohibition. That God rested on the seventh day and prescribed it for the inhabitants of the creation can be passed off as a reasonable and even therapeutic gesture. It is that; and more! God not only ordered rest, She rested. That is more profound than the deity needing or wanting to take a nap! Brueggemann notes that "Rest here means the regular, disciplined, public, visible stoppage of work" (p. 274). The text claims everything not only has its origin in the intentions of God but She can bring everything to a halt. The conventional wisdom is that whatever is, will likely always be. Yet the inherited values, institutions of the world, ethics and morality are subject to God's determination to enact "visible stoppage." Taking a break is comprehensive and consequential. At Her command, covenant partners "cease and desist" and the capacity to self-perpetrate is thwarted. Nothing is permanent but God; nothing else is forever. The orders of the world which appear to be indestructible are at the mercy of the Creator. "Visible stoppage" prevails. Even the coercive is finite. "...Sabbath is a 'divestment' from the ordinary world" (p. 295). In the economy of God the "ways of the world" are terminal even if perceived otherwise.

There is a second theme embedded in the creation narrative not traditionally teased out. God does not need the world and was under no obligation to establish it. There was no hint in the myth that God was lonely or struggling with isolation! She could have gone on enjoying Herself and retaining Her gifts. God did not freeze Her assets but created space for Adam and Eve – and us. Hence, the Divine reality is manifest in generosity; the texture is giving without depletion or reward. God made the world and in time inhabited it in Jesus. Her intent for the world and its inhabitants is that they will replicate the generosity that gave birth to them. God gives and gives and caps Her generosity with

Jesus, even to the cross.

In the economy of God the world exists to be shared; it is not to become a collection of silos. By contrast, one does not need to read *The Wall Street Journal* consistently to be exposed to the merits and necessity of accumulation. It is unambiguously an honorable agenda. And what taps into a stream of anxiety is the query: "Will you run out of resources in your retirement?" The uncertainties of the future culminate in the wisdom of building a "nest egg" for later, uncertainty and insecurity need to be addressed now; after all, "Social Security may not even be there when the time comes." The market economy requires accumulation to function; the economy of God advocates giving after the manner of the Divine Giver. It is not necessary to label greed as the engine of existence; self-preservation is seen as an honorable agenda. Securing one's future has ethical dimensions, even imperatives. It is both noble and necessary. The fear of scarcity translates into organizing life around needs and "the isolated, self-sufficient economic individual" (Brueggemann, p. 375) gets institutionalized. If one does not fuel the system with accumulated assets, eventually it will collapse. Of course, the "invisible hand" is stirring the pot and enabling it to produce goods, even services.

But the economy of God takes form in generosity, giving of self and sharing assets. Accumulation is rendered problematic and less than noble; it is at odds with being in the image of God. And it calls in question the morality of a process gaining sacred dimensions which require it. The generosity of God probes the deification of accumulation and the restrained investment in the needs of others. Again, Brueggemann claims, "The prophetic tradition repeatedly takes aim precisely at the ideology of scarcity and anxiety that produces accumulation aimed at monopoly" (p. 150). At some point it is a theft.

In addition to the Sabbath rest and generosity of God, the economy of God embraces the priority of the neighbor. The boundaries of the self become fluid and even inconsequential. Generosity takes the form of hospitality. Mark Lewis Taylor names God's people a "motley crew" (*The Executed God: The Way of the Cross*) and the church as an "alternative structure" and he notes in the early years of the church hospitality to the neighbor "...was seen as an act of political disobedience" (p. 132). The church is to be a community driven by "...divinely sanctioned practices of love" (p. 132). Associations of care matter! The Egyptians surely were surprised to see God initiate the liberation of their slaves. And Jesus was literally nailed because of his association with the "motley" – tax collectors, prostitutes, the poor and sick, and those who defiled the norms of the day in neighborliness. The Divine Energy is focused consistently on behalf of the neighbor who has been marginalized. The biblical God has an addiction for the lowly and despised whom society ignores. The economy of God holds up their needs at the expense of the privileged. The hospitality of God calls for a "neighborly economy" and that intercepts political and economic power, arrangements which benefit the privileged individual.

The market economy thrives on continuous self-sufficiency. While most would resist the ideology "look out for number one" the reality is that hospitality is appropriate where it serves the needs of the system and the privileged within it. It is painful sometimes to glance over a worshipping community and realize it appears to be a collection of "successful persons" and there is a deficit of "others." Often persons of color, persons gay/lesbians/bi-sexual, those without shelter or supper are not part of the gathered congregation. Hardly the "motley crew" whom Jesus courted. The neighbor is reduced to "our kind;" but not "God's kind"! And it is not simply due to the disposition of individuals but the workings of the worldly order they have created and sustained. God's hospitality is dissolving borders and opening hearts. Again, Brueggemann writes, "A church is to bear witness to a neighborly economy that is an alternative to a market economy of competitive devouring" (p. 268). God's neighborliness is intended to be replicated in the life and mission of the church; and its determination is to call our worldly arrangements that diminish the lives of others, even starve them to death.

The rhetoric and reality of "God's people" in relation to the economy calls for engaging in figurative speech. The faith community, teased into a new creation by straight, white, males is called to affirm the economy of God in subtle ways and leave the "allusions" to be acted upon by the faithful. The ways in which the Bible understands God, gives the Gospel articulation a "bite" and "sting" which assaults the "frozen seas" within us and the social world of our creation. Then, a subversive community is on task. And the breakthrough of God appears.

Bibliography

Brueggemann, Walter. *Ice Axes for Frozen Seas*: *A Biblical Theology for Provocation*. (Waco:
Baylor University Press, 2014.)

Lipsett, B. Diane and Trible, Phyllis. *Faith and Feminism*: *Ecumenical Essays*. (Louisville:
Westminster John Knox Press, 2014.)

Lynerd, Benjamin T. *Republican Theology*: *The Civil Religion of American Evangelicals*. (New York: Oxford University Press, 2014.)

Myers, Ched and Colwell, Matthew. *Our God is Undocumented*: *Biblical Faith and Immigrant Justice*. (Maryknoll: Orbis Books, 2012.)

Oduyoye, Mercy Amba. *Daughters of Anowa*: *African Women and Patriarchy*. (Maryknoll: Orbis Books, 1995.)

Raphael, Melissa. *The Female Face of God in Auschwitz*. (New York: Routledge, 2003.)

Taylor, Mark Lewis. *The Executed God*: *The Way of the Cross in Lockdown America*. (Minneapolis: Fortress Press, 2001.)

West, Cornel and Buschendorf, Christa. *Black Prophetic Fire*.

(Boston: Beacon Press, 2014.)

Whitlark, Jason A. *Resisting Empire*: *Rethinking the Purpose of the Letter to "the Hebrews."* (New York: Bloomsbury, 2014.)

The Relinquishment of Privilege

Within the biblical tradition we have identified two individuals in particular who generate a whisper of promise for straight, white, males. From within an evil empire Pharaoh's daughter was able to sustain enough humanity to secure a future for Moses. Without her cunning the child in a cradle would not have survived the river currents, and the nation of Israel might have been radically different. Then, near the foot of the cross a Centurion called out, "Truly, this was the son of God," naming Jesus while his disciples fled and even the faithful women were at a distance. That discernment was articulated by one of the least likely. The two narratives intersect and establish models of hope which might nourish the prospects for the straight, white, males. While that designation forestalls a lethal encapsulation, some might say it is less than hearty, certainly not liberating. That may not constitute a light at the end of the tunnel but it suggests there could be one at the entrance! Perhaps being in a position of privilege is not terminal or beyond redemption! The break-through of God can even penetrate the Holocaust with the promise of relationality.

Yet we have noted, liberation theologians do not hold out an inordinate amount of hope for those of privilege. And there are some stark texts in Scripture which seem to foreclose on any promise for the likes of rich young rulers, lawyers, and the benefactors of the worldly systems. The "hermeneutical privilege of the poor," skillfully articulated in recent Catholic history, would seem to foreclose any possibility of getting it right. "It is easier for a camel to get through the eye of a needle…" (Matt 19:24) would suggest that the Kingdom is not our destination. Even the prospect of being "born-again" seems less than attainable, unlikely at best!

I

If anyone has written *A Pedagogy of the Privileged*, memory does not immediately surface it. Paulo Freire decoded how our education confronting enculturation can become the means by which the oppressed identify themselves, claim their dignity, and disinherit their circumstances. By contrast Michael Novak has crafted the Catholic tradition so that the market and human initiative are the road maps leading to a life of plenty. If left alone, the system will provide all that they deserve. But where would one look for evidence that the privileged and the system that sustains them are rendered problematic at best and evil at worst? Is it the case that the marginalizers are condemned to a life as victimizers without relief and hope? Is a pedagogy of straight, white, males beyond imagination and redemption?

We are not told much about the Centurion beneath the cross except that he was there and somehow "got it." We do not know if he held on to it! Likely speculation is inappropriate; the data even in a modest degree is simply not present. But what one cannot dispute is that he "got it." It would be a reach to argue he was a straight, white, male; well, certainly a male! And one does not need a major research project to imagine the "military industrial complex" of the day had done its share of indoctrination. The definition of the soldier's experience of that day leaves little room to conclude he was pondering "conscientious objector" status! While everything surrounding him counted against this claim, he declared: "Truly..." He seized the breakthrough of God on the cross. We are not told if it transformed him.

Some lines from Jürgen Moltmann again keep surfacing for some who ponder the problem in the biblical tradition:

Those who hope in Christ can no longer put up with reality as it is, but begin to suffer under it, to contradict it. Peace with God means conflict with the world, for the goad of the promised future stabs inexorably into the flesh of every unfulfilled present.

(*The Theology of Hope*, p. 21)

It would be a stretch to assume the Centurion was planted in the bastion of a Christology. But privilege at the moment did not encapsulate him. The narrative of the crucified and the crucifiers apparently triggers a recognition none would have expected. "Truly..." is rather bold; it suggests "unambiguously", and how could it be read otherwise?

At the end of the previous chapter it was acknowledged that seeing the Centurion as a role model for straight, white, males was not immediately convincing or irresistible. But the event is what it is and may be a cipher for the prospects of the victimizers. Can it be that the contest between privilege and poverty is so stark it is revelatory? Mark Lewis Taylor argues for a kinship between rebellion and revelation: "Rebellion... has a revelatory capacity... [it] creates awareness of these prior conditions... entails a positive flourishing... a kind of resurrection" (*The Executed God*, pp. 156-157). One could reasonably object that rebellion was not personified by the Centurion; or was it? It may be unlikely that he proceeded to spearhead a revolution. But the contrast between his narrative and the one on the cross was stark at best and likely triggered, "Truly..." Rather than in resignation saying, or more commonly during the Holocaust, "you gotta do what you gotta do," he definitely named what God was doing in Christ against the reality of what was being done to him. It is necessary to remember Moltmann did not enter the prison camp a born-again Christian in any sense. His religiosity was marginal at best. Yet in time he wrote, "Those who hope in Christ...."

We hardly need to defend the assertion that the "world" is fashioned to the advantage of straight, white, males. But with the

Centurion some rise out of that, evidencing subtle forms of rebellion that are revelatory and lead to multiple forms of distancing. The social constructions in which straight, white, males live are vulnerable and prone to deconstruction. One can be enabled to see through a different lens. That the oppressed have hermeneutical privileges means the Centurion can undergo a demythologization of sorts, even though the poor have a kinship with Jesus not evident in the privileged.

"Those who again hope in Christ" is a hinge of sorts which leverages access to the event. But hinges swing in two directions, toward the event as it was and toward an accommodation which preempts a counter reality.

It would be fatuous to imagine that in later years the Centurion might have taken a course on the Gospels and then encountered "the Galilean Jesus." At best he could have heard some rumors with hints of that reality in relation to the One on the cross. The fact that there might be a causal relationship between the Galilean Jesus and the Crucified One was certainly a "hint" beyond his scope. But not ours: we may need to search for "the Jesus in context" (Richard Horsley, *Jesus and Empire*, p. 68). Obviously, the Centurion could not have been there! But the point need not rest on the Centurion's exposure. The reality is that context is defining in this and other instances. To say that Jesus was at odds with the dominant order is to frame the obvious. His message of the Kingdom of God proclaims an order different from the prevailing one. "The Kingdom that brings renewal for the people... utterly excludes the people's rule and places them under God's judgment" (p. 79). Justice for the people demands defeat of the ruling regime and its institutions. While Israel has a history of that, it peaked in the proclamation of Jesus. The message of another realm puts the current one at risk. It resonates "with a long Israelite tradition" (p. 89). Nothing is more stark and revealing than that "Jesus was thus symbolically acting out a new prophetic condemnation not just of the building but of the Temple system, because of its oppression of the people" (p. 93). The claim of another King and ruler is subversive of the dominant order.

But it was more than the message of the Kingdom which was subversive. For Jesus it was a lived reality and agenda. He was not a spiritual CEO, whose hands were pitched in prayer, and whose eyes assaulted the heavenly sphere. Efforts to depoliticize Jesus fail. If the Gospels are given a penetrating read, the forgiveness of debts would cut to the economic core of the realm. The very act of returning to Galilee after the crucifixion and resurrection was one of total identification with the resistance to Rome and its Emperor. And before that "Jesus' entry into Jerusalem... [was] a kind of street theatre" (Taylor, *The Executed God*, p. 131) brandishing and provoking Messianic expectations. Galilee was the citadel of resistance to the Empire. Jesus earned his Galilean credentials healing on the Sabbath, elevating the role of women, hanging out with outcasts; all were forms of civil disobedience. The breakthrough of God rippled through his life and ministry. Each act bordered on a dismantling of the social reality created to entrench the Power of the Powerful. Apparently the existing order is "interim" (p. 154).

Now while the Galilean Jesus would be a "draw" for the marginalized and dehumanized today, would it not also be a threat to the regime of straight, white, males? But the Centurion reminds us that distance can be defining; the disparity between the cross and the military regime can be revelatory and point towards rebellion. "The hermeneutical privilege of the poor" need not silence the impulse to say "Truly..." Indeed disparity in its most extreme form can transform a consciousness. The Centurion's declaration is evidence of that – "Those who hope in Christ..." when defined by the "Galilean Jesus" can draw the privileged out of their encapsulation. Even so centered a theologian as James Cone allows for "becoming black," entry into a sphere of solidarity with all its risks and promise.

That "Jesus saves" is not encrusted in the private sphere and linked to a heavenly realm; it enables being "born again" into God's agenda in history. Perhaps the question should be "Whom does Jesus save, where does it transpire, and on what axis does it rotate?"

II

It would be on the far side of problematic to assert that straight, white, males have an advantage in theological agendas. But it would be ironic if in the setting of inclusion one would preclude them! Pharaoh's daughter took advantage of her disadvantage and had the wit to subvert her Father's Empire. The Centurion was smitten by the disparity evident between his military duties and the agenda of the One on the cross. "Truly..." became certainty Jesus was "The Son of God" and upended the imperial agenda. Indeed the purposes of God, far from being defeated on the cross, were fulfilled there as the power of Rome was neutered at the very point it was most strident. And confirmation came several days later. Ironically the state lost in the very act it presumed to win. A soldier "got it" even as the disciples didn't!

To position the event in the setting of the faith community, then and now, calls for collusion between Christology and ecclesiology. While working out the connection for the Black Church in particular, Raphael G. Warnock writes:

From the fledging connection behind the Gospels to the classic debates of Nicea and Chalcedon through the Reformation until now, Christology and ecclesiology have always been done together so that those who are formed by the memory of Jesus must wrestle simultaneously with the implication of that memory for their own mission.
(*The Divided Mind of the Black Church*, p. 1)

More times than not in time the faith community defines the Jesus event, often but not always with some clarity. What is often missing is Christology defining ecclesiology. That does not suggest that the faith community is more important, even more revelatory, than the Jesus event. Rather, that the Jesus event defines who and how the church is meant to be. What this means ultimately is that the church community becomes unafraid to die. It can go to those places and make declarations which are clearly against those in power. Death and apparent defeat do not create a different agenda but the necessity of the perilous one. It is the faith community that declares, "whether we live or we die we are the Lords" not simply a brave soul stoically holding fort. Hence, the agenda of the church is to be the community Jesus was; diversion is a temptation but not an option.

Concurrent with that, the place to be the church is precisely where Jesus was – and with whom! To be a counter community, as Jesus was a public contestant, is to gravitate to the hurting edges of society and up against the structure which perpetuates the wounds. Then, be there as a faith community. Christians should "go to church" to be sent out to the places people are being crucified. It is not enough to write a check, though it helps! The stark reality is that God is not in church unless the church is in the world where "the crucified people" are suffering. The community of straight, white, males has an opportunity for solidarity with those that society has turned against and can be together, "Jesus people" among the broken lives. Being "there" can be transformative and stand up against structure and culture that are breaking. Likely a successful church isn't!

This drives us somewhat gracefully to the issues of God and God's conceptualization. Straight, white, males likely cannot come up with something as stark and consequential as James Cone's claim, "God is Black." That certainly names a location other than our own, and an understanding alien to what he calls the white God. While Cone acknowledges that whites can become Black that does not dictate God's identification or location. White supremacy is thus the agenda of the dominant order and "Speech about God, in the authentic prophetic tradition will always move on the brink of treason and heresy in an oppressive society" (*A Black Theology of Liberation*, p. 56). And the God of the Exodus and the Resurrection is unambiguously identified with "the oppressed of the land." The biblical God embraced liberation as Her worldly agenda. Solidarity is the only hope of those presumed to be faithful. And it poses this question, "Is our God white?" What are the prospects of a traction which would subvert any entrapment in a "White God" and create access to the "Black God?" It is perhaps unlikely that straight, white males will awaken one morning and passionately divest their attachment to a god who authorizes oppression! Yet the Centurion signals that transformation is possible. Perhaps not because of us but because God is not disposed to let us alone! The Gospel of Luke affirms that "what is impossible for mortals is possible for God" (18:27). Brueggemann reminds us that even that barrier can give birth (*The Practice of Prophetic Imagination*, p. 104) and he concludes with the affirmation that the capability of God can "create a newness that defies the categories of the 'possible' that are commonly and reasonably accepted in this world" (p 106). God has an active role in de-privileging the privileged. So, we should step back and as Scripture identifies "wait for the Lord." But "wait" in the tongue of the Bible is an active verb, not a passive one! While anchors have to do with securing our desired positions one can also let go and cast off! And this means, changing location so that we can hear a different word is possible as the "Black God" does not turn white. This means that as the community of faith positions itself where Jesus was – and is now – those within it begin in solidarity with the oppressed to subvert their privileges and say "Truly…" with the Centurion.

III

When reaching back into the origins of a theology rooted in oppression and liberation it is frequently noted that there were rigid silos. Some Black male theologians wrote as if Black women's experience was a replication of their own. Some White feminists wrote as if color did not constitute uniqueness in the confidence women's experience is not divisible. And the Third World versions of oppression were seldom taken into account, in fact not discovered much less honored. In time, fortunately, the recognition of intersectionality emerged. While oppression is destructive but divisible it is undergirded by a common reality in all its formation. In many that was articulated as economic in origin. The intersectionality is driven by common forces and the instances of oppression can only fully be dissolved if this is recognized. And it was.

Intersectionality is evident in the phenomenon of straight, white, males. And while they are named in consort each has an ideological silo. But what is evident and destructive in all this is a sense of entitlement. And where it is not evident, it is sought. While entitlement is perceived as earned it is owned in a way it becomes not simply a privilege but a right. It is exclusory in nature and diminishes any claim of others upon our privileges. And relinquishment is not desirable because it would open one to vulnerability. As a straight, white, male one is not required to let go; it would divest oneself of a shield. In another context (American exceptionalism) Walter Brueggemann refers to it as a "totalizing ideology" ...[that] takes the form of 'chosenness' of the white western superiority that guarantee privilege and preclude serious change" (p. 131). Any dismantling of the shield of straight, white, males would leave one at risk to the interests of the "other." The ownership of a straight white world banishes the claim of another. Brueggemann quotes Martha Nussbaum in regard to those open to other yet resistant to them. And she explicitly identifies "the tendency to seek domination as a form of self-protection, versus the ability to respect others who are different…" (p.144). Ironically it is a world that is gone even as some are confident it is permanent.

And this underscores the issue of relinquishment, letting go of what sustains privilege. What might enable straight, white, males to relinquish their form of domination? For at least a brief moment the Centurion experienced relinquishment when he declared, "Truly…" What triggered the demise of a "false consciousness?" What would enable what Brueggemann calls a "counter-imagination?" to protrude (*Truth Speaks to Power*, p. 89)? That is grounded in "the boundary-crossings, authority-defying freedom of God" (p. 104). Relinquishment grounded in a Divine interaction and an occasional spontaneous, "Truly…" But the relinquishment has a community as a setting which is not singular and dependent upon individual interaction. Brueggemann quotes Michael Walzer:

> First, that wherever you live, it is probably Egypt. Second, that there is a better place, a world more attractive, a promised land; and third that the way to the land is through the wilderness! There is no way to get from here to there except by joining together and marching. (*The Practice of Prophetic Imagination*, p. 148)

God is not trapped in the heavens; She has impregnated the earth in "the Galilean Jesus" and liberation can occur in a community that "got the hint" has become possible. The liberation of privilege is finally the result of this breakthrough of God… embraced.

Bibliography

Brueggemann, Walter. *The Practice of Prophetic Imagination* (Minneapolis: Fortress Press, 2012).

Brueggemann, Walter. *Truth Speaks to Power*: *The Countercultural Nature of Scripture* (Louisville: Westminster John Knox Press, 2013).

Cone, James. *A Black Theology of Liberation* (Mary Knoll: Orbis Books 1986).

Horsley, Richard. *Jesus and Empire* (Minneapolis: Fortress Press, 2003).

Moltmann, Jürgen. *The Theology of Hope*: *On the Ground and the Implications of Christian Eschatology* (New York: Harper & Row, 1967).

Taylor, Mark Lewis. *The Executed God* (Minneapolis: Fortress Press, 2014).

Warnock, Raphael G. *The Divided Mind of the Church* (New York: New York University Press, 2014).

Index

Circle Books

CHRISTIAN FAITH

Circle Books explores a wide range of disciplines within the field of Christian faith and practice. It also draws on personal testimony and new ways of finding and expressing God's presence in the world today.

If you have enjoyed this book, why not tell other readers by posting a review on your preferred book site. Recent bestsellers from Circle Books are:

I Am With You (Paperback)
John Woolley

These words of divine encouragement were given to John Woolley in his work as a hospital chaplain, and have since inspired and uplifted tens of thousands, even changed their lives.
Paperback: 978-1-90381-699-8 ebook: 978-1-78099-485-7

God Calling
A. J. Russell

365 messages of encouragement channelled from Christ to two anonymous "Listeners".
Hardcover: 978-1-905047-42-0 ebook: 978-1-78099-486-4

The Long Road to Heaven
A Lent Course Based on the Film
Tim Heaton
This second Lent resource from the author of *The Naturalist and the Christ* explores Christian understandings of "salvation" in a five-part study based on the film *The Way*.
Paperback: 978-1-78279-274-1 ebook: 978-1-78279-273-4

Abide In My Love
More Divine Help for Today's Needs
John Woolley
The companion to I Am With You, Abide In My Love offers words of divine encouragement.
Paperback: 978-1-84694-276-1

From the Bottom of the Pond
The Forgotten Art of Experiencing God in the Depths of the Present Moment
Simon Small
From the Bottom of the Pond takes us into the depths of the present moment, to the only place where God can be found.
Paperback: 978-1-84694-066-8 ebook: 978-1-78099-207-5

God Is A Symbol Of Something True
Why You Don't Have to Choose Either a Literal Creator God or a Blind, Indifferent Universe
Jack Call
In this examination of modern spiritual dilemmas, Call offers the explanation that some of the most important elements of life are beyond our control: everything is fundamentally alright.
Paperback: 978-1-84694-244-0

The Scarlet Cord
Conversations With God's Chosen Women
Lindsay Hardin Freeman, Karen N. Canton
Voiceless wax figures no longer, twelve biblical women,
outspoken, independent, faithful, selfless risk-takers, come to
life in *The Scarlet Cord*.
Paperback: 978-1-84694-375-1

Will You Join in Our Crusade?
The Invitation of the Gospels Unlocked by the Inspiration of
Les Miserables
Steve Mann
Les Miserables' narrative is entwined with Bible study in this
book of 42 daily readings from the Gospels, perfect for Lent
or anytime.
Paperback: 978-1-78279-384-7 ebook: 978-1-78279-383-0

A Quiet Mind
Uniting Body, Mind and Emotions in Christian Spirituality
Eva McIntyre
A practical guide to finding peace in the present moment that
will change your life, heal your wounds and bring you a
quiet mind.
Paperback: 978-1-84694-507-6 ebook: 978-1-78099-005-7

Readers of ebooks can buy or view any of these bestsellers by
clicking on the live link in the title. Most titles are published in
paperback and as an ebook. Paperbacks are available in traditional
bookshops. Both print and ebook formats are available online.

Find more titles and sign up to our readers' newsletter at
http://www.johnhuntpublishing.com/christianity.
Follow us on Facebook at
https://www.facebook.com/ChristianAlternative.